A BRIEF HISTORY
OF IMBECILITY

D1601276

A BRIEF HISTORY OF IMBECILITY

Poetry and Prose of Takamura Kōtarō

Translated by Hiroaki Sato

UNIVERSITY OF HAWAII PRESS

Honolulu

Library of Congress Cataloging-in-Publication Data
Takamura, Kōtarō, 1883–1956.
[Selections. English. 1992]
A brief history of imbecility : poetry and prose of Takamura
Kōtarō / translated by Hiroaki Sato.
p.   cm.
Expanded ed. of: Chieko and other poems of Takamura Kōtarō.
1980. With new introd. and prose essays added.
ISBN 0–8248–1405–3 (cloth). — ISBN 0–8248–1456–8 (paper)
1.   Takamura, Kōtarō, 1883–1956—Translations into English.
I.   Sato, Hiroaki, 1942–   . II.   Title.
PL817.A43A27   1992
895.6'144—dc20   92–11916
CIP

Frontis: Kōtarō with his bust of Kōun, his father, in 1911.

University of Hawaii Press books are printed on acid-free paper
and meet the guidelines for permanence and durability
of the Council on Library Resources

CONTENTS

Poems

PART I: THE JOURNEY

Contents

Contents

Contents

Prose

Contents

TRANSLATOR'S NOTE

This is an expanded edition of *Chieko and Other Poems of Takamura Kōtarō*, published by this press in 1980, with thirteen prose essays added. The Introduction is new and is partly based on my speech at "Paris in Japan," a conference held by Humanities West in San Francisco on January 14, 1989; the speech was then serialized in my column for the *Mainichi Daily News*, "Here & Now—in New York."

The translations of some essays are partial. The omitted portions are usually indicated by ellipses dots or the absence of section numbers. I have held down to the minimum the notes on the artists and literary figures mentioned in the essays, though I have supplied some personal and family names without so indicating.

In prose, Takamura was often surprisingly awkward: at times, perhaps, because the public stance he took made him unduly self-conscious, as in "A Green Sun"; at other times, because the subject was difficult, as in some parts of his piece on his wife, Chieko. In translating such pieces I have chosen to give, as best I could, the flavor of the original writings by not smoothing out the infelicities. This I have done against the advice of Robert Fagan who, as always, has expertly edited my translations along with the rest. However, my attempt to be faithful to the original texts does not extend to Takamura's often overly long paragraph formations, which I have shortened arbitrarily.

All the English and other foreign words and phrases Takamura used in the essays are retained and italicized. The brackets contain the translations of the preceding word or words or the notes on them.

Where Takamura refers to years by those in the eras of Meiji, Taishō, and Shōwa, I have retained them rather than converting them into their A.D. equivalents. For those unfamiliar with those eras, Meiji lasted from 1868 to 1912; Taishō, from 1912 to 1926; and Shōwa, from 1926 to 1989.

In addition to Robert Fagan, Nancy Rossiter and Eleanor Wolff have provided editorial help.

This book is dedicated to Michael O'Brien.

INTRODUCTION
Takamura Kōtarō and Paris

In December 1910 Takamura Kōtarō (1883–1956) wrote a
brief poem called "The Country of Netsuke" which contin-
ues to affect Japanese of older generations with great force:

Cheekbones protruding, lips thick, eyes triangular, with a face
    like a netsuke carved by the master Sangorō
blank, as if stripped of his soul
not knowing himself, fidgety
life-cheap
vainglorious
small & frigid, incredibly smug
monkey-like, fox-like, flying-squirrel-like, mudskipper-like,
    minnow-like, gargoyle-like, chip-from-a-cup-like
Japanese

Why was Takamura railing at his compatriots? What was
the reason for his anger, frustration, and despair? The short
answer to the question is: his Paris experience.

Takamura Kōtarō was born the first son of Kōun and
Waka (later, Toyo). Kōun (1852–1934), a wood sculptor spe-
cializing in Buddhist objects, was at the time in considerable
poverty. As Kōtarō recalled much later in *Kaisōroku* (Mem-
oirs), an interview prepared at the height of World War II,
Kōun, unable to earn enough money in the profession of his

choice, made papier-mâché and other festival trinkets and, for foreign traders, wooden models for things like "*matroos* [sailor] pipes, inkstands, handles for Western umbrellas, knives, clock stands, and mirror frames," which included, Kōtarō added, "disgusting things likely to please the Westerners."

Kōun's financial difficulty may have been in part a reflection of the time. After making the historic decision to remove the restrictions on international commerce in the mid-nineteenth century, the Japanese government opted for wholesale Westernization in the first phase of its effort for *bunmei kaika*, "civilization and enlightenment." This meant denigration or dismissal of most things Japanese. Also, as the imperial system was restored, Shintoism replaced Buddhism as the national religion.

But about the time Kōtarō was born, a reaction toward the opposite extreme set in—the swing of the pendulum that would help change the course of the Takamura family. Ironically, one important advocate of reemphasis on Japan's indigenous culture was a non-Japanese, Ernest Fenollosa (1853–1908). Fenollosa, a Harvard graduate who had come to Japan to teach political economy at the Imperial University of Tokyo, in 1888 founded, with Okakura Tenshin (1862–1913), the Tokyo School of Fine Arts for the exclusive purpose of teaching and promoting traditional Japanese art. The following year Okakura persuaded modest Kōun, who felt teaching at a school was too exalted for him, to join the faculty. A year afterward, when professorships were created at the school, Kōun was promoted to professor of sculpture; he was also appointed a member of the Imperial Art Board. In time he would be decorated with the Second Order of Merit and accorded junior third rank.

Kōun was accomplished in his trade. In 1893, at the Chicago World's Fair, his wood sculpture entitled *Old Monkey*

Introduction

won a grand prize. He also made two of the best-known bronze statues in Japan: the equestrian one of the legendary warrior Kusunoki Masashige (1294–1336), which stands on the Imperial Palace grounds, and the one of the statesman Saigō Takamori (1827–1877), which is in Tokyo's Ueno Park. Some years after Kōtarō's death the sculptor Takada Hiroatsu, who knew Kōtarō well, wrote that these statues of two great national heroes were the finest examples of this genre in Japan.[1] This judgment would have discomfited Kōtarō, as we shall see.

Kōtarō trained under his father to be a sculptor, first at home, then at the Tokyo School of Fine Arts. By the time he began to attend the art school, the pendulum was swinging in the other direction, with hostility to Western art softening considerably. In 1897, the year he was admitted to the school, Kuroda Seiki (1866–1924), a painter with ten years of study in France behind him, was employed as the first professor of the newly created section of Western-style painting.

Kōtarō was at the school for more than eight years. In September 1905, when he switched to the section of Western-style painting, he had among his classmates Fujita Tsuguji (1886–1968), who would go on to become "one of the few Japanese painters working in the Western manner to have an international reputation."[2] By then Iwamura Tōru (1870–1917), professor of Western art history and aesthetics, had persuaded his senior colleague, Kōun, that Kōtarō should study abroad. Iwamura's words to him, "Your son Kōtarō is a masterpiece far superior to any of your works," are believed to have pleased rather than offended Kōun, who was by all accounts an exceptionally generous man.

In February 1906 Kōtarō left Yokohama for New York. He arrived at Grand Central Station about a month later, but the two New York sculptors to whom Iwamura had written letters of introduction did not accept him as an assistant. Luckily Gutzon (also spelled Gutsom) Borglum (1867–1941), later of Mount Rushmore fame, hired him. In the meantime he attended the Art Students League of New York, where he won second prize in an annual competition. The prize freed him from having to pay tuition for the following year. But Kōtarō did not stay. With the special prize of seventy-five dollars that Borglum, an instructor at the school, gave him, he moved to London in June 1907. The idea in those days was to work and make some money in New York before going to Paris for serious study. But Kōtarō does not seem to have been overly impressed by what he saw in New York, either, or in London, though in both cities he was an indefatigable student of art and language. Paris, where he lived from June 1908 to May 1909, was different. The city was spellbinding to him and profoundly changed his outlook on life and art.

The reason was obvious: Paris then was the artists' center of the world. Everyone with artistic aspirations assumed this. New York and London may have boasted some impressive museums, but not much else. It was easy, even natural, for Kōtarō to report from New York, as he did in his letter of October 22, 1906, that at the Art Students League he almost quarreled with his instructor every day, and that even though he found this turn of events "endlessly fascinating," it came about because he "dislike[d] extremely the vulgar, what you might call the American, taste."

Kōtarō was never that high-handed about Paris. He was exhilarated by everything he saw and experienced—while in a perpetual state of doubt and despair. In a group of "Letters Left Unmailed," which he published after his return to Japan, Kōtarō spoke of the constant need to remind himself that he was now in Paris; so engrossed was he in chasing strange and beautiful things, he said, that at times he forgot it would hurt if he pinched himself. The primary cause was, of course, art—above all, art as exemplified by Auguste Rodin.

Kōtarō's first and fateful encounter with Rodin went back several years, to 1903, when he saw a photograph of his sculpture, "Poesy." Albeit in reproduction, it is thought to be the first Rodin that was introduced to Japan. Its impression upon Kōtarō was so strong that he jotted down in his diary, "What a master!" Two years later he bought an English translation of Camille Mauclair's book, *Auguste Rodin*, and reread it so many times he almost memorized the whole text. In New York he chose Gutzon Borglum in part because Borglum had been influenced by the French sculptor.

Now in Paris he saw an exhibition of several hundred drawings—all of nude women—by Rodin. Though aggrieved to feel that he did not possess the kind of "animal electricity" that the master had, Kōtarō was moved beyond "simple words."

In another unmailed letter he wrote: "When I see Rodin's sculpture a flower blooms in my heart. If no one were around I'd sleep holding his marble *Nymphe*. I feel like Rodin's women are actually made from my ribs. I can't for the life of me believe that he *made* them. Rodin is someone who's holding a plough and digging the earth. He's someone who knows what's buried where. He's someone who digs it up and brings it to the people. He's a broker who exists between nature and man."

Rodin's influence on Kōtarō was decisive, as is evident to anyone who looks at his sculptures before and after his sojourn in Paris. As an art critic back in Japan, he used the presence or absence of *la vie*, apparently a Rodinesque term, as a vital criterion. He published two selections of Rodin's words in his own translation, as well as a biography of the sculptor. He was of course keenly aware of the danger of becoming a second-hand imitator and, probably because of this self-consciousness, he did not in the end make many bronze sculptures. Still, he, along with Ogiwara Morie (1879–1910), who likewise came under Rodin's profound influence and did some powerful work before his premature death, is thought to have laid the foundations of modern sculpture in Japan.

("Modern sculpture," as opposed to traditional Japanese sculpture, is a concept Kōtarō struggled to clarify and establish. What the term ultimately meant to him is not clear, even though the art historian Takashina Shūji has suggested that for Kōtarō the distinction of modern sculpture may have lain in being "non-utilitarian."[3] What fascinates us in the context of Japan's modern intellectual struggle with the West is that Kōtarō came gradually to recognize that Rodin, the supreme artist, and his own father, a *mere* craftsman, emphasized some similar basic points in executing a sculpture. In addition, in making the much admired wood sculptures he carved later in his life, Kōtarō used and cherished the skills he had learned from his father when young.)

If Paris exhilarated Kōtarō with its heightened artistic atmosphere, it also made him despair. The source of his despair was a racial inferiority complex.

In a famous piece entitled *Cafe yori* (From a café), which he published a year after returning to Japan, he narrates a sexual encounter he had in Paris. One seductive evening in Montmartre, he runs into three fun-loving Frenchwomen. Things work out in such a way that he ends up spending the night with one of them. "I thought I had never tasted the freshness of skin as well as on that night," he thinks.

The next morning he awakens before his female companion. While he is savoring the very French landscape that spreads outside the window, the woman wakes and opens

her eyes. What beautiful blue eyes! "Through the windows
of those eyes one can see the indigo blue of the sky over the
Indian Ocean," he muses. "One can see the transparent color
of the Aegean Sea reflecting marble. Fragments of the
stained glass from the Cathedral of Notre Dame. The color
of the shadow of Monet's forest. The mysterious color one
sees in the dark *saphir* in the treasure house of a *mosquée*."
While he is lost in such poetic reverie, the woman urges:
"Now, let's get up. Let's get up and have some breakfast." So
he jumps up and saunters off to the wash basin. Here's the
rest of the account:

> When I was turning on the hot-water faucet, I didn't mean
> to, no, I didn't—but I looked up: standing there was an unfa-
> miliar, dark man in a nightgown. An extreme unpleasant-
> ness, unease, and alarm simultaneously assaulted me. I
> looked closer, and it turned out to be a mirror. It was I who
> was in the mirror.
> "No, I am Japanese after all. I'm *Japonais, Mongol, le
> Jaune!*" a voice cried out in my head as if some mechanism,
> wound up too tight, had broken.
> At that instant my dreamy state of mind collapsed like an
> *avalanche*, its roots and all. That morning I ran away from
> the woman as soon as I could. And sitting for a long time on
> the cold wooden floor of my studio, I went through some
> painful thoughts.

This racial inferiority complex, coupled with his ineradi-
cable conclusion, given in one of his "Letters Left Un-
mailed," that "the white race is a riddle that will never be
solved," made Kōtarō cut short his stay in Paris to less than a
year. He had initially planned to be there for several years or
more.
In June 1909 he arrived back in Japan, a land he had
longed to return to but at the same time dreaded, as he put it
in another "Letter Left Unmailed," as "a dry, tasteless soci-

ety like a Sparta with its art uprooted and taken away from its life, where people go about in kimonos so short as to expose their shanks and sit around on tatamis overgrown with mold." He became a member of the Pan's Club, a group of self-styled "decadent" writers and artists, and frequented Yoshiwara brothels, at one time fighting with a friend over a prostitute, whom he called Mona Lisa. He became a scourge to the art world. His article, "A Last Glance at the Third Ministry of Education Art Exhibition," published in January 1910 and regarded as the first full review of this kind in Japan, is also a model of sarcasm, which is delightful to us now but must have been infuriating, painful, even destructive to the artists whose works became Kōtarō's targets.

As might be expected from someone impatient with the discrepancies between what he upholds as the ideal and what he sees as the reality, Kōtarō, while severely criticizing his fellow artists, promoted Western art and poetry with dedication. He translated and wrote about a great number of European and American writers and artists. To list only those whose words, poems, and ideas he published in book form, they are, in addition to Rodin: van Gogh (his sister Elizabeth's "Memoirs," 1921); Walt Whitman ("Diary Excerpts," 1921); Emile Verhaeren (*Les Heures claires*, 1921; *Les Flammes hautes*, 1925; *Selected Poems*, 1953); and Romain Rolland (*Liluli*, 1924). Kōtarō also wrote book-length surveys of art, one a history of Impressionism, and another an overview of modern sculpture. In his posthumously published eighteen-volume "complete works," articles on art and literature take up seven volumes, translations three.

Perhaps because he gave so much energy to his missionary urge, for a number of years he was not a prolific poet. Still, his first collection, *Dōtei* (Journey), published in 1914 with money his father gave him, went on to become one of the two landmarks in modern Japanese poetry, showing a mastery of colloquial language for the first time. The other is *Tsuki ni Hoeru* (Howling at the moon) by Hagiwara Sakutarō (1886–1942), which came out in 1917.[4]

What were the consequences of the racial inferiority complex that Kōtarō himself described so starkly and the admiration for Western culture he tried so doggedly to show? Two things that happened would become crucial to his life and work: his wife's madness and his turn to jingoism.

In 1914 Kōtarō married Naganuma Chieko (1886–1938), an aspiring painter and a member of the *Seitōsha*, a group for women's liberation established three years earlier by Hiratsuka Raichō (1886–1971).[5] The marriage was based on a resolve to pursue the kind of artistic integrity and sexual equality that Kōtarō had observed in the West, especially Paris, and which Chieko knew amply about. As the couple led their artistic life together in an expensive atelier Kōun had built for his son, the pursuit of the two values seemed not to produce noticeable mishaps for quite a while, even though there certainly were some inconveniences. Adherence to artistic integrity in Kōtarō's case took the form of a refusal to take a job with a guaranteed income and an avowed reluctance to make sculptures for sale. As a result, he was from time to time forced to "borrow" substantial sums of money from his father. For Chieko the stress on sexual equality meant having her own studio and Kōtarō sharing the household chores. Also, since Kōtarō did not enter her name in the family register at marriage, as far as Japanese law was concerned she was not his wife. She had freedom as an artist and as an individual. The outwardly uneventful life lasted for a dozen or more years.

But then Chieko started to show symptoms of schizophrenia. After a series of hallucinations and depressions, she attempted suicide, in 1932. Some treatments were tried, but in time she began to behave violently, cursing and throwing things at Kōtarō; she would break out of the nailed doors and harangue the neighborhood, sometimes from atop a tall fence. For three years Kōtarō nursed her, feeding and bathing her "like an infant" when he could. In the end the physical danger of living with Chieko overcame his determination, and in February 1935 he put her in a hospital, where she died three years later.

As may be discerned from Kōtarō's own account, "The Latter Half of Chieko's Life," the causes of schizophrenia were not well understood then, and in fact researchers today are still trying to sort them out. But even if it is established someday that the disease is caused by physical and biological rather than environmental factors, Kōtarō may not have been entirely misguided in feeling that their pursuit of Western ideals strained Chieko's none too strong nerves.

Out of his life with Chieko, Kōtarō produced his second selection of poems, *Chieko Shō* (Excerpts from writings about Chieko), published in 1941. For Kōtarō, who started to write about Chieko while courting her, her death in madness, let alone writing about it, was of course something he could not have possibly foreseen. That makes all the more poignant his obvious dedication to the Belgian poet Emile Verhaeren, who, in *Les Heures claires*, a sequence of poems extolling his love for his wife, had written the following lines:

Alors, oh! serrons nous comme deux fous sublimes
Qui, sous les cieux cassés, se cramponnent aux cîmes
Quand même—et, d'un unique essor,
L'âme en soleil,
S'exaltent dans la mort.

Introduction

Then, oh! let us clasp one another like two sublime lunatics
Who under broken skies hold fast to the summits
None the less—and, impelled as one,
Souls sun-radiant,
Are exalted in death.

(Translation by Eleanor Wolff)

Kōtarō's dedication to Verhaeren—some have noted his translations of the poet, for their polish, as among the best Japanese translations of European poems—has prompted some critics to complain that Kōtarō fictionalized his relationship to Chieko, modeling it on that of Verhaeren to his wife. It has also been said that Kōtarō "beautified" that relationship. But such complaints are idle. Varied in mood, precise in image and presentation, *Chieko Shō* deserves to be what it has continued to be since its publication: the longest-running best-seller in modern Japanese poetry. The example that best shows Kōtarō's skill as a poet is also the most famous of all his poems, "Lemon Elegy":

So intensely you had been waiting for lemon.
In the sad, white, light deathbed
you took that one lemon from my hand
and bit it sharply with your bright teeth.
A fragrance rose the color of topaz.
Those heavenly drops of juice
flashed you back to sanity.
Yours eyes, blue and transparent, slightly smiled.
You grasped my hand, how vigorous you were.
There was a storm in your throat
but just at the end
Chieko found Chieko again,
all life's love into one moment fallen.
And then once
as once you did on a mountain top you let out a great sigh
and with it your engine stopped.

Introduction

By the cherry blossoms in front of your photograph
today, too, I will put a cool fresh lemon.

If Chieko's madness, along with the shadow it cast, is one
of the two determinants of Kōtarō's life and work as seen in
relation to his experience in Paris, the other is his gradual
turn against the West and submission to jingoism. About the
time Chieko showed the first schizophrenic symptoms,
Kōtarō's views of art began to take on nationalistic overtones
and, as Japan's expansion of its war against China in the
thirties became the frequent target of worldwide criticism,
he became more nationalistic in his writings, both prose and
poems. Particularly after the Pacific War began, Kōtarō
became one of the strongest advocates in the literary and
artistic world for Japan's militaristic policies. As though his
earlier racial inferiority complex had been stood on its head,
the admirer and promoter of Western ideals turned himself
into a facile user of trite, tawdry, and dangerous military
slogans such as *Kichiku Beiei*, "Demons and Beasts, U.S.,
U.K." And as this happened, a man who in 1910, fresh from
his Paris experience, had accused his compatriots of being
"life-cheap," "vainglorious," and "incredibly smug," ended
up urging them—in a "vainglorious," "incredibly smug"
manner—to hold their lives "cheap" in order for Japan to
carry out its "holy war."

Chieko's schizophrenia was for Kōtarō a private ordeal.
In contrast, his turn to jingoism had social consequences
which, to some, were extremely grave. A few months after
World War II ended in Japan's defeat, the literary critic
Odagiri Hideo frontally attacked Kōtarō's "unprecedented,"
"despicable" change in stance, his "degradation." Noting
that "with a blinding speed as if tumbling down a cliff, the
poet fell, only to turn into a megaphone" for the Japanese
militarists, he charged him with "war responsibility" of the

Introduction

"first order."⁶ Largely in response to the accusation, Kōtarō "exiled" himself from Tokyo and lived in a ramshackle house in a remote village in northern Japan for seven years after the war. At the beginning of the self-imposed removal from the cultural center, he also wrote an apologia of sorts, a sequence of twenty autobiographical poems called *Angu Shōden* (A brief history of imbecility).

Since then, Kōtarō's apparent change or changes of heart have been a subject of literary criticism, speculation, and contemplation, providing the focal point for much of the discussion on Japan's Westernization and the relationship between Japanese literature and World War II. As a result, almost all imaginable analytical venues have been tried. My attempt to account for Kōtarō's life—at least that part where he tried to digest European culture and tradition and, in some way, failed—from the viewpoint of a racial inferiority complex itself takes its cue from the literary critic Yoshimoto Takaaki's famous article published in 1957.⁷ Nevertheless, some points may deserve review and further thought.

During the intense period of Westernization many Japanese became open admirers of social and cultural manifestations of the West. That is certain, but this does not mean that in doing so they permanently shunted aside their own social and cultural roots or forgot their national consciousness. In the case of Kōtarō, his younger brother Toyochika pointed out that in some of his writings, such as the poem "Sculpture Only," he played down his interest in the outcome of Japan's war with Russia. It was such a momentous national event, Toyochika thought, that it could hardly have left Kōtarō so detached.⁸

Indeed, Kōtarō was enough of an old-fashioned nationalist to decline to evacuate Tokyo for months during the concentrated bombings of the Pacific War, saying, incredibly to Toyochika, "As long as His Majesty resides here, I am not

Introduction

going to leave."[9] By then, of course, he, as a poet and artist, was spearheading what were proving to be disastrous militaristic ventures. But his sense of himself as a Japanese did not come to the fore suddenly during the thirties, or for that matter the forties. Throughout his life Kōtarō kept recalling how while in New York he had picked fights with Americans who called him "Jap" and got the best of them. This form of insult galled him in part because, one gathers, it was just after Japan's victory in its war with the Russian empire.

There is another angle from which to look at Kōtarō. When he thought he had run into a cultural dead end in France, he decided not to stick it out but to go back to Japan, a country of which he despaired. His decision or willingness to abandon what was, for him, an important culture at the beginning stage of what would later be termed "culture shock" meant acceptance of an incomplete understanding of the West. He was a well read, well educated, and highly observant man; nevertheless, for quite a while after returning from France, he would typically make observations like this:

True, even in the households of ordinary Japanese today there are many who live among tasteful hobbies of their own choosing. Nō chanting, flower arrangement, tea ceremony, koto, etc.—there's nothing lacking. But the odd phenomenon is that in many cases there's absolutely no relationship between this cultural training and the daily lives or the internal lives of those who engage in it. In other words, when they look to the right, they forget what's to the left, and when they look up, they forget what's below. The tea ceremony lives only in the world of tea ceremony, and the koto seems to live only in the atmosphere of koto. Some of the skilled people who have received a "diploma" in flower arrangement have no idea of form. Some who do traditional dance can take mysteriously silly photographs. All this is probably

Introduction

because in many the so-called self isn't alive, working to make the individual's entire life an organic whole. So, when a couple of skilled "ladies" turn up, people are astonished as if they're a miracle or something. I once saw in London a low-class female vendor polishing her nails. This may have been an exceptional example, but I thought this was an interesting country where the awareness of beauty is more developed than the notion of "gentleman" or "lady."[10]

Here Kōtarō may be right—but only up to the point where for comparison he conjures up what he saw in London: in his haste to express his despair or contempt for his compatriots' failure to understand "culture" in the proper fashion, he insouciantly extrapolates overall European cultural sophistication from a glimpse of "a low-class female vendor polishing her nails." This is the sort of error of comparison that someone like Mori Ōgai (1862–1922), Kōtarō's teacher at the Tokyo School of Fine Arts and later his colleague in a literary gathering, would never have made in his laxest moment. Ōgai, in fact, is known to have pointed out once that Kōtarō's idea of "self" *(jiga)* was deficient because it did not presuppose the existence of "the other" *(taga)*.[11]

Admiration based on such half-baked understanding was bound to prove vulnerable. As domestic and international turmoil mounted and Japan's sense of international isolation increased from the end of the First World War to the beginning of the Second, Japanese admirers of Western notions began to be forced to realize and resent—like someone trapped in an unrequited love—that those who embodied them did not necessarily look upon their supplicants kindly.

For example, in his long unfinished novel, *Ryoshū* (Travel melancholy), the modernist Yokomitsu Riichi (1898–1947) made his alter ego, Yashiro, reflect: "For a long time Japan has learned various things from Europe. At the same time, because of this, Japan has been made to endure constant humiliations from Europe." With this thought, Yashiro feels like "a soldier marching into a battlefield" as his ship approaches France. Much of the novel is based on Yokomitsu's six-month experiences in Paris and elsewhere in Europe in 1936. A few days after Japan's assault on Pearl Harbor in 1941, Kōtarō expressed similar sentiments in a poem called "Brilliant Winter":

> The world has been renewed once and for all.
> Time has arrived for settling all the accounts since the
>   Black Ships.
> The development of a race has made it possible.
> For a long time pushed around,
> pooh-poohed, juices squeezed,
> we've even held masked balls,
> we've learned from them everything we could,
> measured their strength from one end to the other,
> and fully appreciated their dirty-mindedness.
> Now the day's come we can return to the old,
> go back to the spring,
> and turn into a torrent that runs a thousand miles a second.
> The reason our race exists in the world
> for the first time takes definite form in people's eyes.
> Bulbuls are calling, it's winter.
> Sasanquas are falling, it's winter.
> But it's a brilliant winter when, yesterday a remote past,
> even nature has revived itself.

Finally, it may be worth reflecting that there was something about World War II that turned the normally intelligent into willing nonthinkers and uncritical upholders of government-sponsored goals—in Japan and elsewhere. As Paul Fussell has recently described it, with the approach and outbreak of the Second World War, an "ethically purified atmosphere," a "self-congratulatory mode," and "unmitigated high-mindedness" prevailed with astonishing ease, and an "outpouring of patriotic drivel" ensued, in the United States and Britain.[12] At least in Japan, the United States, and Britain few writers seem to have come out of the horrendous war with their moral statures undamaged, unscarred.

Fashions change. Someday it may be possible, as has been suggested by the literary critic Hirakawa Sukehiro, to expect a reevaluation of Takamura Kōtarō's wartime poems from viewpoints not taken so far by the majority.[13] Kōtarō certainly has left us a great many of them—the poems in his third, fourth, and fifth books are mostly such pieces—and a considerable number may withstand poetic analysis. Yet, poetry does not exist in a vacuum in any age, and sentiments sympathetic to Homeric pronouncements for valor and sacrifice will be a long time reviving in poetry, if not in tabloid writings, so it is doubtful that many of Kōtarō's nationalistic poems written during the thirties and the first half of the forties will begin to be included in anthologies any time soon.

But the value of many of the other poems that Kōtarō has left us is unlikely to change with time. His ability to capture the essence of the moment—we may call it *la vie*—was extraordinary; his ability to describe it with precision, even more so. And, though certainly not without limitations, he had a great mind.

About one-seventh of Takamura's poetry is represented in this volume. Part 1, "The Journey," while bearing the title of his first book of poems, consists of fifty-eight chronologically arranged pieces chosen from all periods of his life. It includes "Italian Pilgrimage" (a brief travel account with haiku), "From the Workshop: II" (fifty tanka accompanied by a letter), and "15 Occasional Pieces" (a selection of epigrams). Excluding the one cited above in full, only one overtly nationalistic poem, "To General Kuribayashi," is translated.[14]

Part 2, "Chieko," is made up of twenty-six poems selected from the more than forty pieces about her and arranged in the order of their composition. Despite their apparent simplicity and spontaneity, many of these poems were composed months and years after the events.

Part 3, "A Brief History of Imbecility," is a complete translation of the sequence of twenty poems mentioned earlier. As noted, Kōtarō probably intended these poems to be an apologia; but what he actually wrote proved to be a moving account of a life in the most turbulent decades in modern Japan.

The thirteen essays that follow the selections of poems— some translated partially, some wholly—are intended to show Kōtarō's principal artistic concerns and interests as they were formed and changed. These pieces—some youthfully anxious and questioning, some exuberantly harsh, some gentle, mature, and reconciliatory, but each invigorated by Kōtarō's unmistakable poetic eye—range from letters he wrote while in Paris in 1909 to musings on the traditional Japanese sculptor's tools that he wrote while in "exile," in 1950.

Of these, three essays—on the Japanese sculptor Ogiwara Morie, the American sculptor Gutzon Borglum, and Chieko —may at first glance seem somewhat out of line, but these are included to add human dimensions to some of the arguments Kōtarō makes elsewhere in a more abstract fashion. Especially "The Latter Half of Chieko's Life," a participant's account of the struggles of two artists in the first part of this century, still has a great deal to tell us, I believe, as the century draws to a close.

NOTES TO THE INTRODUCTION

1. Takada Hiroatsu, *Takamura Kōtarō to Chōkoku* (Takamura Kōtarō and sculpture), *Gendaishi Tokuhon* 5 (Tokyo: Shichōsha, 1978), p. 173.

2. Laurance P. Roberts, *A Dictionary of Japanese Artists* (Tokyo: Weatherhill, 1976), p. 26.

3. Takashina et al., "Takamura Kōtarō no Sekai" (The world of Takamura Kōtarō), *Eureka* Special: *Takamura Kōtarō* (Tokyo: Seidosha, 1972), p. 124.

4. *Dōtei* includes "The Country of Netsuke," quoted at the outset of the Introduction, as well as the poem entitled "——N Joshi ni" (——To Miss N), which some have called the first successful poem free from traditional 5- and 7-syllabic patterns and skillfully employing the vernacular. The latter was later revised and its title changed to *Hito ni* (To someone).

For Sakutarō, see my complete translations of *Tsuki ni Hoeru* and his second book of poems, *Aoneko* (Blue cat), in *Howling at the Moon: Poems of Hagiwara Sakutarō* (Tokyo: University of Tokyo Press, 1978).

5. Hiratsuka remained an activist for women's rights throughout her long life. Her motto was "In the beginning the woman was the sun." Her sense of humor can be discerned in the name of her group, which may be translated as the "Association of Blue Stockings."

6. Odagiri Hideo, *Takamura Kōtarō no Sensō Sekinin* (The war responsibility of Takamura Kōtarō), originally published in January 1946. Included in *Gendaishi Tokuhon* 5 (n. 1 above), pp. 166–167.

7. Yoshimoto Takaaki, *"Dasazuni shimatta Tegami no Hito-taba" no koto* (On "A Bundle of Letters Left Unmailed"). Since it was published in the monthly newsletter accompanying the first of the 18-volume series of Takamura Kōtarō's "complete works" from Chikuma Shobō, it has been reprinted in a number of collections.

8. Takamura Toyochika, *Teihon: Kōtarō Kaisō* (Definitive edition: Remembering Kōtarō) (Tokyo: Yūshindō, 1972), pp. 31–32 and elsewhere.

9. Ibid.

10. *Kōbō Zakkan* (Random thoughts in a workshop), published in February 1911.

11. Kawaji Ryūkō quoted Ōgai's remarks in his conversation with Kōtarō in *Ōgai Sensei no Omoide* (Remembering Ōgai Sensei), originally published in *Shi Seikatsu* in January 1939.

12. Paul Fussel, *Wartime: Understanding and Behavior in the Second World War* (New York: Oxford University Press, 1989), pp. 164–180.

13. Hirakawa Sukehiro, *Takamura Kōtarō to Seiyō* (Takamura Kōtarō and the West), *Shinchō*, December 1989, p. 9 and elsewhere.

14. A supplementary selection made for this expanded volume would have added a few similarly nationalistic poems, but the selection had to be discarded for reasons of space. It is scheduled to be printed in *Pembroke Magazine* in 1993.

Poems

THE COUNTRY
OF NETSUKE

Cheekbones protruding, lips thick, eyes triangular, with a
face like a netsuke carved by the master Sangorō
blank, as if stripped of his soul
not knowing himself, fidgety
life-cheap
vainglorious
small & frigid, incredibly smug
monkey-like, fox-like, flying-squirrel-like, mudskipper-like,
minnow-like, gargoyle-like, chip-from-a-cup-like Japa-
nese

NIGHT IN A STUDIO

The fire in the stove's gone out,
from the four corners of the room, unnoticed,
the cold sneaks up like electric current.
The brightness of a silk cape, unblinking,
has robbed things of yellow.
The way this cluttered studio is so lonely!
As I think of someone who still smiles in my mind
paint and canvas become a game
—Art is no more than repeating clever conventions—
I'd rather deride the paintings of Chavanne
and weep over a glass of liqueur.
The cold is harsh
at two o'clock on a winter night.

DESOLATION

The red dictionaries
funeral-march,
the fireless stove
listens to a cuckoo's voice ringing over a mine,
the wrestler Onogawa's lament
lurks in the floral design of a soiled carpet.

Someone comes
and pours phosphorus, steadily
into the frosted windowglass, steadily—
at this moment dusk spills red ink by mistake.

Where should I run?
There's nowhere to run.
What should I do?
There's nothing to do.
I can't sit still.
Threat fills the earth.

Unaware I wrap myself in white flannel
and, in my heart, the exhaustion of a steam bath,
dream persistently of the principle of electromagnetism.

The red ink pad, whitened with dust,
derides today's black star, the day of the Buddha's death;
while the barometer causes great disturbances,
the moon, losing weight, floats on the sea.

Crane perfume remains silent on an envelope,
somewhere, beaten in punishment, weeping
a barmaid screams.

Ah, tell me the road I should run,
let me know what to do,
the bottom of a glacier, like fire, hurts,
it hurts, it hurts.

MY FATHER'S FACE

When I make my father's face with clay,
below the window in twilight
my father's face is sad and lonely.

Its shadings, having some resemblance to my face,
are eerie, the law terrifying,
and the old age of my soul, nakedly
manifest, unexpectedly startles me.
My heart, eager to see what it fears,
looks at the eyes, the wrinkles on the forehead.
My father's face that I made
remains deeply silent like fish
yet tells, alas, of its painful days of the past.

Is it the dark cry of steel
or the ghost's voice of *Hamlet* I saw in the West?
Its piercing echo, though without rancor,
seeps into my nails and throbs like whitlow.

When I make my father's face with clay,
below the window in twilight
the mysterious lineage of the blood whispers . . .

ITALIAN PILGRIMAGE

These are the useless writings that I jotted down in my diary four years ago when I left Paris to see Italy, so my conscience suffers a bit. But because of the heat I hope you'll excuse me.

* * * * *

The Swiss city Lucerne, at the end of March, still has remnants of unmelted snow, and the Alpine mountains surrounding it and Quatres Cantons, the lake that opens up in front, darken quietly, quietly like the breathing of a girl reading the Bible.

> The aged corridor of Kapellbrucke—the hexagonal building of Wasserturm—
> In the transparent blue water tiny fish are looking for tonight's resting place.
> Bells ring—Ave Maria echoes on the mountains and water.

The women of this mountain country are affectionate and kind. At the Hotel de la Cloche, my lodging house, a warm supper must be ready by now.

Yet, in this summer resort, the lamps of the casino by the lake, now closed and lonely, more than attracted my heart.

Still more, wasn't there a blonde city girl hurrying home with her mother, talking about young English nobles coming here soon with the summer?

Please do not think I was being melancholic. My heart was dancing more lightly than you would imagine.

I shave, how cold the spring in Switzerland

On a rock a Christ sits, how cold

What mountain is it, and what river, in the haze

Evening glow, the glaciers do not flow away to the lower
world

After dinner, I drank bock while listening to an ensemble
of winds and strings in an aristocratic restaurant.

The quiet of the Swiss night was as transparent as ice.

Today I boarded a "saloon boat" with about ten passengers, crossed the lake, Quatres Cantons, and landed at the village of Flüelen. On the water I suspected people's taste at "Tells Kapelle" and also envied some interesting log cabins. The white walls of a church in Flüelen glistened like ivory chessmen. Immediately at the back were gigantic mountains.

Dominating the church tower, what mountain is it, in snow?

Still, the sunlight reflecting on the lake had something familiar about it. Serenity of heart while waiting for the train.

On the lake oil undulating, it's a long day

Then the train enters the celebrated St. Gotthard Tunnel. Having an extraordinary fear of tunnels, I felt as if I were actually buried under the ground. Deep in my heart and at the back of my skull I felt the weight of the earth.

When we finally came past the mountain territory it was already early evening, and the snow was falling, flickering playfully.

Italy! At last I've come to Italy.

Coming out of the tunnel, it's snowing at the border

And the train runs along the shore of Lake Lugano and the shore of familiar Lake Como. Already hotel cabs for travelers could be seen waiting at each station.

> Snow-melting spring—flower-blooming spring—and the summer when cool winds blow—summer in which lively young men delight—

The train goes on running.

With what a lachrymose heart the eyes used to mountains, rocks, forests, and waters looked out the train window at the plains of Lombardy and the urban-looking village roofs.

The mountains of the Alps, dyed pink and mandrill-red, mark the distant horizon. In a small village an orange market was set up. The oranges were probably the first, arrived to-day from Sicily in the south.

> Even a woman with lipstick's buying the summer oranges
>
> Glistening, through the burnt field and long, the railway
>
> Willows already, pears at long last, are green
>
> More rutilant than the roof of a holy building, the spring snow
>
> Chimneys are visible in the distance, in the spring field
>
> Snow melts, an utterly ruined mansion, relics

Sun already set, about the time you could no longer distinguish faces clearly, the train stopped quietly at the station of Milan. It stopped, composed, as if greatly relieved.

I hired a cab and drove out into the streets. It was a spring evening. This morning I was on the mountains. Now I was going down the grand avenues of Milan. There was a wind hinting perfume.

And the black hair of women—

That night I thought of resting my tired body at a hotel near the main church, but, mind enticed, I went to see an opera at La Scala and couldn't stop a traveler's dreamy licentiousness.

Then too, there was a spring rain as light as alcohol.

Spring rain, a scarlet slip and a black umbrella

Tiptoeing, a maiden goes in the spring rain

My face reflects in the window, a spring evening

The house full of women look at me, this spring night

In the morning I left the hotel and climbed to the roof of the main church. Remembering a chapter in *The Improvisatore* I once had read, I was moved to tears. With a red-covered guidebook in my hand, and horse-drawn, I spent several days, sightseeing west and east. Leonardo da Vinci's wall paintings are here. So are his drawings. I put almost all my mind to various museums and libraries, and to studying basilicas.

Nevertheless, when the dazzling electric lamps glittered, I never forgot to visit the bar, Gambrinus, and to stop in the cross-shaped gallery with a glass roof, Vittorio Emanuelle, halfway down the street.

Spring night, honeyed words and painted looks, virtue rare

I too stare back at the women, this spring night

A traveler's mind is always pressed. In early April, after lunch, I left this great Milan, becoming again a passenger. I was heading for the city of Padua in the east.

The Lombard plains continue endlessly.

I was born and saw Milan, spring wind

11

Looking at the expansive Lombard plains, the traveler was lured into poetic sentiments that arose somehow. Half asleep, half awake, he let the velvet window curtain play with his face.

Sleeping face handsome, a woman, in spring's train

Spring water flows in a small ditch

That evening I arrived in the Padua of Dante and Giotto. It was a rustic-elegant countryside city, lonely, yet full of light and power.

A rain fell on streets that looked good under rain.

At night I drank red wine in the dining hall of the hotel. And I adored the butter pats shaped like ancient medals. The woman who guided me to my bedroom along deep corridors had a candle in her hand. The floor boards of the corridors faintly echoed our footfalls.

"*Buona sera, signor,*" the woman said, and it sounded archaic. I wondered if she called herself Francesca so-and-so.

At night I wrote letters with much feeling. For a blotter, they had provided a pot of sand.

Ah, Padua of Dante and Giotto.

Spring, from time to time, the rain is cold, I travel alone

The next day it cleared up, then it rained again. I spent the day reading quietly and resting.

Morning clouded, I look out the window at pear blossoms

Enter the old town of Padua, an apple market

Then, for several days I walked about, following my feet, and looked at every nook and corner of this small famous city.

The archaic buildings with stone columns standing on both sides of the streets delighted me a great deal. The cob-

12

blestones of the carriage ways were worn and fiercely uneven, and the roof tiles of some houses looked ready to fall at any minute. Yet even these didn't seem so bad.

Among others, the holy Il Santo absorbed my soul, and Dante's house wouldn't let me go easily.

> Entering the church, the cold of the stone, spring rain
>
> A woman going to confession on a rainy April day
>
> Spring rain, Dante once lived in this house
>
> Donatello's horseman is blue, spring wind

Above all, what thrilled my heart was Giotto's famous wall paintings, *The Life of Christ*. The sensation I felt when I pushed open the door of the shed-like Madonna dell'Arena and stepped in the dim room was almost that of facing great danger.

The fresco's slightly faded indigo sky—trees—birds— Christ's sparkling eyes—the meaning of folds—the power of silence—

And the painter's modesty.

> Spring rain, Giotto's wall paintings, colors faded

About the time Padua's horse fair was over, I went east again.

Soon I came to the sea. The train ran a long bridge. I saw gondolas. I reached an island.

It was Venice.

> Swaying onto a gondola, spring evening
>
> Shall I get an Italian woman, this spring evening
>
> A beauty praising oysters, on her cheek an artificial mole

COMPLAINT

It's so frustrating,
you won't even beat me up—
if you're a man,
why don't you act like one?
What's so hot about grinning all the time?
That's dumb.
Now, take Otome's old man,
he drags her around by the hair, so I hear.
If I turn my back on you, why don't you beat the hell out
    of me?
Why not grab me by the throat till I can't breathe?
You're such a weakling, a boneless wonder.
You don't mind taking insults from your wife.
You're such a frustrating man.
If I was you,
damn it, I'd tear the clothes off me, tie me up tight with a
    hemp rope,
hang me from the ceiling,
put burning tongs to my flesh,
beat, thrash me till I whimper.
You don't have the guts for that, do you? Whatever I say
    to you,
whatever I do to you,
all you do is yes-yes.
You never hit back.
Or do you think you can't come up and swat me?
Look, a woman's a woman, you know that.
If you got serious about it I wouldn't be able to do a thing.
You can't get serious, can you?
So if I lean on you, you make a sour face and clam up.
You milksop.
Or do you think the minute you bully me I'll run away?

If you do, you don't understand anything.
Look at Otome.
She's got bruises for every month,
since they moved here, it's almost three years.
I envy her.
And that reminds me, her old man's got more than meets
     the eye.
Where are you in comparison?
All you think about is snoring away and feeding your face,
you don't hate me or love me, one way or the other, do you?
If I didn't speak up, you'd sleep a whole month with your
     back turned away, wouldn't you?
Are you really a man?
Like Buddha's statue in Ueno, Lord knows what you're think-
     ing.
Come on, man, pull yourself together.
I don't give a damn for my life.
If you get mad
do whatever you like with my body.
Tie me to the rack and see what'll happen.
Sit on me and rub pepper all over me, and see what'll hap-
     pen.
Ah, I hate it, I hate it,
you wouldn't even *dream* of doing anything like that.
Your wife insults you, says foul things to you, but you pass
     it by, don't you?
If I make you a cuckold, you might perk up a bit.
Look, I love you.
So I wouldn't mind your killing me, that's what I'm saying.
But, *do* something.
Lord knows, you *are* frustrating.
You don't even beat me up—

15

WINTER HAS COME

Determined, winter has come.
The white flowers of the eight-fingers gone,
ginkgo trees have turned into brooms.

The piercing winter that twists into you has come.
The winter nobody likes,
the winter betrayed by grass and trees, spurned by insects,
   has come.

Winter
come to me, come.
I winter's power, the winter my prey.

Seep through, penetrate,
cause fires, bury in snow.
Blade-like, winter has come.

CLAY

A cold winter mist
pleasingly covering the town
brought off a pretty scumble on the street lamps that night.
Feeling like I was walking around under waves let loose,
nervous
I was walking, looking at the lights, that night.
Suddenly my heart became clouded,
I remembered the clay I was working on,
a female torso.
My steps immediately got confused.
Ah
I've wasted time irretrievably,
I thought
and became angry, unbearably.
I almost rammed myself, as I jumped on a streetcar.
I hurried back, tumbling forward,
to my studio, dark, out of town.
It was dark,
cold, spacious,
I couldn't see a thing.
On the windowpanes dewdrops had formed,
stars twinkled.
To me, that midnight the studio
wasn't as scary as usual.
I turned on the lights.
The torso I was working on had a white cloth covering it.
I sat on the model's platform
and tried to calm myself.
I had done all I could.
Today, until the minute I let the model go
I did my best.
There was still something further,

but nature as I saw it was surely mine.
After the model left
I recall how I washed my hands quietly,
looked at the clay and smiled:
a heavy, soft female torso
a bursting round power
large arched chest
stomach as broad as the base of a mountain
navel as deep as a well
snappy pelvis tips
nipples as small as a dove's chest
warm, dark armpits
blade-bones on the abundant shoulders
buttocks like two lovely moons
untroubled, friendly, absurdly fat thigh flesh
bold, delicate cleft in the groin
and running from bottom to top
a bundle of power that wells up cozily
terribly erotic, terribly noble female flesh—
I don't forget the smile I smiled.
I don't forget the exhilaration of the moment when my pre-
        vious works salaamed before it.
I don't forget how, washing my hands
when I looked at the clay,
my feet began to dance, of themselves,
and stepped, abandonedly,
a polka march, double time.
I don't forget any of this.
Thinking of it
I couldn't understand why that anxiety,
like some predicament,
like some terrible omen,
threatened me.
At any rate
I rose to my feet and removed the white cloth.
Light struck the clay.

I held my breath and stared at it.
Fool, fool, fool,
what is this hard, tinlike affair?
A crab shell?
An acorn shell?
Seedy, wizened, dumb,
empty,
a hodgepodge,
a lump of ramble-scramble mud!
"Accidental" modeling, so?
And this banality,
awkward banality,
you bungler!
I was furious.
I was mortified.
Standing, I folded my arms.
I felt unbearably lonely.
That loneliness shook up my reality.
I couldn't stand still.
The nature I felt welled up and danced before me.
Am I no good, no good?
Am I a man who commits suicide?
Am I an incompetent, a weakling?
If I know clearly that I have no bud from which my life
    grows, I'll kill myself.
That's what my conscience commands me to do.
Am I? Am I?
Am I such trash?
Am I afraid of nature insulting me,
of confronting nature?
The loneliness became a terror.
The terror became again a loneliness.
Tears dropped in drops.
They went down my cheeks.
I am weeping—as soon as I noticed it,
in tears I began to sob.

My own tears angered me,
truly angered me.
I didn't at all feel like sleeping that night.
I sat on the chair again,
looked up at the clay, as if shouting at it.
I found a large crack on the torso's back.
My nerves really trembled.
Ah, is someone going to destroy this,
destroy me?
I jumped up.
Like a bitch protecting her puppy
I protected the clay.
Come what may, come, I decided.
And I peered into each of the four dark corners of the studio.
Each had only darkness stuffed in it.
A sigh came out.
I picked up a spatula.
And I poked at the crack and patched it up,
placing a piece of wood for support.
I pressed on it,
fumbled at it with my fingers.
Fumbling,
I still felt a lump in my throat.
When the bellies of my fingers and the clay, sticking to each
    other,
were kneaded,
I began to feel a certain power,
I began to think that I was close to the clay,
I began to think that my fingers knew the clay,
began to think that the clay delighted in me.
I shuddered like a warrior before battle.
I'll make something, something out of this pitiful torso.
I'll grow, I'll grow up.
I'll surely enliven this clay.
I'll surely enliven nature.
I'll pursue it to the end.

The clay whispered to my fingers:
Turn back to your mission.
It whispered: The job laid on you is immense.
I agreed, with all my body.
I am a man who, by nature, can't help making life.
Make, make, make with all your power.
While making, rejoice and sorrow.
While making, get angry and get lonely.
To make is to walk forward.
To make is to live.
One step, and another step.
Don't tarry.
Push on.
Thrust forward.
I again looked vividly at the real female flesh.
Look, look at the day
when this clay revives.
I shave life and fatten life.
I put back the white cloth.
That night I fell asleep without taking off my socks.
When I woke,
white frost glistened on pine needles
and the sun grew up from the horizon beyond the field.
I gazed at it.

THE JOURNEY

Before me, no road.
Behind me, a road.
O Nature,
Father,
Spacious father who made me stand on my own,
Do not lose sight of me, protect me,
Fill me always with a fatherly spirit,
For this long journey,
For this long journey.

AUTUMN PRAYER

Autumn rings gaily in the sky
the sky is aquamarine, birds fly
the soul neighs
clear water flows through the heart
the heart opens its eyes
and becomes a child.

The past, with its many edges and dusty details, lies before
    me
it is the source of my blood.
Bathed in autumn light, I quietly look at what there is,
I bless the lives under the ground,
survey, deeply moved, the way I have come,
I rouse, I pray:
I pray not knowing the words
in tears
beaten by light
I see leaves fall,
see beasts running joyfully,
see flying clouds, in the garden grass blown in the wind
and seeing these rhythms of cause and effect
feel in my heart strong obligation and love
yet think of the endless compunctions as well,
unbearable,
and in joy, loneliness, and dread, I kneel:
I pray not knowing the words,
I look at the sky and pray,
the sky is aquamarine
autumn rings gaily in the sky.

CLEARING SKY

Don't know since when it's been raining,
lukewarm dank mire
dark overhanging rainy December day.
Abruptly, out of nowhere
from some distant high point, splashing the rain,
comes a cold wind.
At once the trees cringe,
through the rustling world
nonchalantly a streak of wind blows.
Undulating their hair mussed up from sleeping
the clouds step out of their languorous beds
and in irregular lines,
in heaven, try to shake off sleep.
The wind torments the rain,
the wind rages at everything,
and blowing, sweeping, baring,
tears into pieces the heaven-filling clouds.
At that moment
beyond the horizon
heaven tears slightly
and light green light
shines in joyously.
Soul delighting in the cold wind,
I run out into the field,
every piece of mire on the road glistens,
pools quietly reflect the green in heaven.
The fierce wind blows still harder
and harder,
and now the world is ready to be purified.

CAT

So, you want to eat rats that much,
black cat Sechi.
Wearing luxurious fur no lady owns,
all night long
in the dusty attic
you keep still, hardly breathing.
Is it so pleasurable,
so irresistible
to catch live things?
Ah, what is this,
what is this?
Black cat Sechi,
you are beautiful the way you are,
endlessly beautiful.
But what is this terror that persists in my heart?

MELON

Sent by a florist friend in Fujisawa, a small box,
I raised the lid, the inside was packed with bog moss.
Pleased as if solving a puzzle
I pulled the moss away
and a huge melon rolled out
onto the floor struck sideways by morning sun.
A rock-stout, huge, light yellow melon,
the fossilized bladder of a mammoth from centuries ago
    perhaps,
it looked like a baseball for the gods.
A net of veins running in every direction covered it.
I held it up, it was weighty.
Its look was comical, or dead serious.
I took out Leach's large plate with a blue picture,
put it under the morning window,
raised the melon reverently in both hands, and thumped it
    down.
Green leaves' reflection—
like a surgeon, a sharpened knife in hand,
I cut into it.
Contrary to what I'd thought, it sliced softly, noiselessly.
Ah what beauty, quietness:
the pink flesh of the melon wrapped in thick courteous rind
the peach color of a dove's breast
dawn on a mountaintop
"Robin Adair" in the mist
the healthy upper arm of a pioneer's young daughter.
I did indeed pile up glittering pieces of ice
and set out a silver spoon
but at the wonderful sight on the plate with a blue picture
my heart was shaken

and in the room full of the rough fragrance of the fresh
   melon,
breathing the green morning light,
I couldn't begin to touch it, marveling, until the people I
   called arrived.

CATHEDRAL IN THE THRASHING RAIN

O another deluge of wind and rain.
Collar turned up, getting drenched in this splashing rain,
and looking up at you—it's me,
me who never fails to come here once a day.
It's that Japanese.
This morning
about daybreak the storm suddenly went violent, terrible,
and now is blowing through Paris from one end to the other.
I have yet to know the directions of this land.
I don't even know which way this storm is facing, raging
over the Île-de-France.
Only because even today I wanted to stand here
and look up at you, Cathedral of Notre-Dame de Paris,
I came, getting drenched,
only because I wanted to touch you,
only because I wanted to kiss your skin, the stone, unknown
to anyone.

O another deluge of wind and rain.
Though it's already time for morning coffee,
a little while ago I looked from the Pont-Neuf,
the boats on the Seine were still tied up to the banks, like
puppies.
The leaves of the gentle plane trees shining in their autumn
colors on the banks
are like flocks of buntings chased by hawks,
glittering, scattering, flying about.

The chestnut trees behind you,
each time their heads, spreading branches, get mussed up,

28

starling-colored leaves dance up into the sky.
By the splashes of rain blowing down, they are then
dashed like arrows on the cobblestones and burst.
All the square is like a pattern,
filled with flowing silver water, and isles of golden-brown
burnt-brown leaves.
Then there's the noise of the downpour resounding in my
pores.
It's the noise of something roaring, grinding.
As soon as human beings hushed up
all the other things in Paris began at once to shout in chorus.
With golden plane tree leaves falling all over my coat,
I'm standing in it.
Storms are like this in my country, Japan, too.
Only, we don't see you soaring.

O Notre-Dame, Notre-Dame,
rock-like, mountain-like, eagle-like, crouching-lion-like
cathedral,
reef sunk in vast air,
square pillar of Paris,
sealed by the blinding splatters of rain,
taking the slapping wind head-on,
O soaring in front, Notre-Dame de Paris,
it's me, looking up at you.
It's that Japanese.
My heart trembles now that I see you.
Looking at your form like a tragedy,
a young man from a far distant country is moved.
Not at all knowing for what reason, my heart pounds
in unison with the screams in the air, resounds as if terrified.

O another deluge of wind and rain.
How furious these four elements of nature
that would, if they could, snuff out your existence, return
you to the original void.

Smoking phosphorescent shafts of rain.
Scales of the clouds flying, mottled, not quite touching your
    top.
Blasts of the persistent clinging gales, trying to snap off at
    least one column of the bell-tower.
Innumerable, small, shining elves that bump against the
    rose window dentils, burst, flow, and flap about.
Only the gargoyles, the monsters on the high architectural
    rims, visible between splashes,
taking on the flitting flocks of elves,
raise their paws, crane their necks,
bare their teeth, blow out burning fountains of breath.
The many lines of mysterious stone saints make eerie ges-
    tures, nod to one another
the enormous arc-boutants on the side reveal their familiar
    upper arms.
To their many arms that form arcs aslant,
O what a concentration of wind and rain.
I hear the reverberation of the organ during Mass
How is the rooster at the tip of the tall slender steeple doing?
Flapping curtains of water have dammed up all directions.
You stand in them.

O another deluge of wind and rain.
A cathedral standing in it
solid with the weight of eight centuries,
a mass of many millions of stones piled and carved by be-
    lievers of old.
A great scaffold for truth, sincerity, and eternity.
You stand wordless,
you stand, taking on, motionless, the force of the blasting
    storm.
You know the strength of nature's force,
have the composure of mind to leave yourself to the ram-
    pant wind and rain, till the earth shakes.
O rusty gray iron-colored skin of stone glistening in the rain.

My hands touching it
feel as if they were touching Esmeralda's white palm.
And along with Esmeralda, the monster
Quasimodo who delights in storms is hiding near some mold-
ing.
A just soul crammed into an ugly body,
a firm strength,
silently absorbing on his back
the words of those who wounded, those who whipped, those
who would do wrong, those who despised, and not to
say the least, those who were petty,
he ground himself to serve God,
O only you could give birth to that monster.
How many non-hunchbacked, non-deformed, more joyful,
more daily Quasimodos
have been born since then
and nurtured on your breast full of solemn, yet protective
motherly love, and gentle.

O Cathedral in the thrashing rain.
Baton swung down abruptly at the sudden
turn of the wind and rain that took a breath and has driven
itself harder,
all the instruments of the heavens gone berserk,
the dance swirls around them.
O Cathedral, you who at such a moment keep ever more
silent and soar,
Cathedral, you who watch motionless the houses of Paris
suffering the storm,
please do not think me rude,
who, hands on your cornerstone,
has his hot cheek pressed on your skin,
it's me, the drunken one.
It's that Japanese.

WOODEN CLOGS

Only the ground, a threshold, and boxes of salted crackers
    are visible.
From the window of the streetcar that's stopped in a narrow
    street,
it's good heavens a miserable filthy cracker shop,
but left at its threshold are the three pairs of clogs.
Among them is a pair with red straps
of tiny mini-clogs just bought,
set neatly like a treasure.
The winter morning sun is shining warmly on them.

FROM THE WORKSHOP: II

Quite unusual for the summer, I've been working hard, not
becoming weak. My energy has kept up so well, it seems, be-
cause early in the summer I hitchhiked about the Deep Jōshū,
visiting a few spas in the mountains. It seems that one of the
spas had a particularly good effect on me. It seems that the
bubbles of the spa endlessly welling out of the ground tossed
in me something elemental and vital. I remember the rock
floor and the bubbles with delight. Few things in the world
are as delightful as spas. But spas with hot water drawn from
elsewhere, as in Ikaho, are no good. They feel dead. Mrs.
Yosano presented me with her *Meteor's Way*, and I felt deep-
ly honored. Other friends and strangers have given me their
books and magazines. I'm thinking of writing my impres-
sions of them sometime soon. I'll also write soon what I felt
looking at the fall exhibitions. About sculpture, I didn't make
money from it, so I couldn't study models during the precious
summer. I regret it but can't do a thing about it. So I came up
with this idea of a club for distributing my small wood pieces
and put an ad in the September issue of *Myōjō*. If I have a few
members every month, I should be able to use models. I'd
been doing wood carving intermittently since childhood, but
around February this year I took it up seriously. I'll keep the
sea robin, my first work this year, as a memento. Recently
I've been making various insects. The beauty of a tiny thing is
something else. It has a strength subtle and unexpected. With
clay, I'm now making four heads. This year I've come up
with useless tanka from time to time. I have my own reasons
for them, but since they're the kind of tanka which Mr. Yosa-
no, our teacher, will reject if I show them to him, I decided
just to abruptly jot down about fifty recent pieces in these
pages which I consider are given to me. Though I burn for

"poems," in writing tanka I again feel as delighted as a child. In tanka I now wish to step forward from the kind of reality hidden behind "poems."

Ceaselessly, hurriedly, climbing up a cherry tree, the cicada stops and begins to sing

Breaking off, the *min-min* starts over again, how bright its death song

Finishing its song, the *min-min* immediately flew up and bumped into the ball, the evening sun

Because it's droning away single-mindedly, I don't feel like collecting the cicada with my bag, I just look at its belly

The children gave me one of their cicadas. I'm so delighted, even while eating supper

As the sizzling squeaking sound of a cicada grows clearer, it becomes inaudible to the ear, it simply fills the sky

Summer-day song that resounds and drones in heaven, its singer is a solitary tiny cicada

Abruptly it raises its voice *ji-ji* and falls silent again. Sad cicada, cicada in a cage

It has nothing of the squalor of living things, it's dry and light, this brown cicada

I put the cicada on my hand, it doesn't even try to fly; sluggishly, itchingly, it crawls around the palm

What shall I give this cicada of which I can't tell where its mouth is? I have nothing to give

Modestly crawling on my hand the tiny cicada says *ji-ji* and swiftly flies into the blue sky

When it flew up the cicada scratched my hand; I can't forget the power of its legs

Having finished whetting all the knives, I am carving a cicada in shifting evening twilight

As I carve its wings and its eyeballs, the wooden cicada breathes, hushed, and crawls in evening twilight

Motionless, until this, this piece of wood, decays, the wood-carved cicada stays on

Though a small bug, it'll live longer than I, I think, my lovely cicada

Under the electric lamp I look at the wood-cicada; I do not tire of looking at it, a mere bug, a cicada

Cicada with its wings folded quietly, touched so often the wings gleam a little

I whet my chisels and cut wood. Knowing that in my heart, I feel wasted

Cypress fragrance moving everywhere in the room, summer rain gleams at the blade tip of my pointed knife

Holding a triangular woodchip, I draw lines with ink—they are so dear, the cicada's eyes

I asked him to collect stag beetles—he, Ozaki Kihachi at Takaido, must be doing so tonight as well

Holding a stag beetle's antlers, my friend must be looking at them, surprised

Resounding reverberating lives fit the mud of the rough earth, which I make heads out of

Though it softly touches my fingers, it may be sighing deeply and grieving, this slime

On this summer day are you at a milestone looking at a horse or taking a nap, Prince Yamawaki?

A naked gecko's body transparent, on the windowglass the moon has inclined

As I try to carve them from wood, the naked gecko's lovely babies go to sleep in my bed

When I pick up the gecko's baby it's all eyes, undulating its throats, trying to get away

When your father is alive and your mother is as well, how sad to make poems of them

Stripped naked I write a summer poem—does Verhaeren take a peek at it?

Single-minded, headlong, I work—don't think I'm lonely, Chieko

Look at this man: Verhaeren, because he loved his wife as I do, made things without stopping

Majestically something like water flowing fills the sky, flowing through my heart

When I'm exhausted and go to your room on the second
floor, I want to eat things like a little boy

Bear's-strawberries, on a mountain cliff in Deep Jōshū, eating
them alone, I become a bear

Though I'm quiet, as soon as I leave man's realm, I ride a
mountain wind

What is it but the slough of myself that's mingling in the
human realm?

To tell you honestly, I belong to the family of quadrupeds
that live on a wild mountain like this

I'm not what's called a beast but a creature totally new

Soaking my body in natural hot water I hear a secret agent's
remote underground voice

In a corner of a roomy rock bathtub, dark and immersed is a
daughter of Echigo

The little daughter stealthily washing her mother's back,
clothed herself with steam and went away

The bubbles that run up from the bottom rock, the bottom
pebbles, cling to my skin and don't go away

You better forget about human beings—though I'm not say-
ing it, a mountain wind blows

Now it's so funny to think about the man—when I become an
animal and soak in hot water

Though it's a long way over mountain paths, if there weren't
people looking, I would have come holding Chieko,
who's in the city

Mountain crows are cawing for the evening; from the rock
bathtub in the valley faint steam rises

I wet the dry edge of red rock with hot water, rise splashing,
and sit on it

INTEGRITY

Barely visible, transparent, crystalline weasel
at soaring crag-blasted mountaintop
takes a deep breath
leaps on a twister that swoops up the valley
and three thousand miles out
lies low under fallen cherry leaves in the autumn city,
clanks on the pavement—
touch it, in broad daylight it'll slit your skin.
Ah, this daemon's soul, too sharp,
ever-unaccommodating, how lonely, how maddening, how
        unstoppable!
Blowing away the mist of loving kindness
cutting light winds of emotion
now behind you
now to your right
turns on itself, again, determined, it rushes.
Not a soul ahead of it
drunk with solitude, holed-up in solitude
it chews on tree fungus
spits at the human world.

Ah uncontrollable integrity,
nails sharpened by the northwester that comes from the
        horizon,
tears its own flesh
lets blood drip
bathes every day in the welling underground fountain
makes waterdrops shine silver.
Drenched with too much of humanity
it tramples opportunity
expunges comfort
swiftly hides itself in the void—

ever-unaccommodating, the transparent crystalline weasel
nurtures itself in the ocean the indigo green,
again, in a flash, goes back
to that mountaintop air.

POLAR BEARS

In windswept Bronx Park with the remains of snow like
    coarse sugar,
face mute, a typical Jap,
he stands on a precious Sunday before the cage of the polar
    bears.

The polar bears too, silent, occasionally look at him.
The polar bear, just when you've decided it's too sluggish,
leaps buoyantly, body trembling smashes the ice, and
    splashes the water.

Sharp icicles hang at the cave made of rock,
shine prismatically
on his head, play continuously a fury-like livening pirouette
    rhythm.

After taking care of the rent out of his seven dollars pay,
he has left in his pockets a few coins that are stamped with
    an eagle and make a noise.
Hands tucked in his pockets, he keeps his mouth shut.

Two big polar bears come out of the water
and, undulating their backs straight as the Arctic horizon,
noiseless, they walk about on the frozen concrete:

dead-honest flat forehead, pinkish greedy lips,
frost-and-snow limbs and body concealing splendid power,
and small, alien, phosphorescent eyes.

Leaning on the fence, cold wind clouting his ears,
in the bleak ice-field of the spirit,
he burns a heart joyful without cause, and valorous.

41

The polar bear, finally, doesn't give itself to man,
burdened inside with the cross of ferocious instincts
it breathes Northern seas, alone in a New York suburb.

The baseness of cozy refinement fills his surroundings.
A suffocating gratuitous Christian materialism
is about to kill a dreamer, a Jap.

The polar bears too, silent, occasionally look at him.
Not hearing "All right" for the first time in a week,
washed in silence, he stands before the vast polar bears.

HEAD-HUNTING

I want a head,
a head that sits so well you can't budge it with a lever,
a head fragrant with spring orchids,
a head you can hold like a balloon,
a head you would put on a silver tray and consecrate to the
    morning table,
a totally different head, a gust of wind,
a classic head full of dreams and polished with intellect,
a head, charged electrically, hushed, before a storm,
a beauty's head that torments Mephistopheles,
but after all, the head of a man,
a head which you can plonk down, just like that,
a head which is, nevertheless, unfathomable and innocent,
I'll hide a dagger in my pocket
today too, and mingle in the city crowd.

ONIONS

The onions sent by a friend in Tachikawa,
stretching their two-foot white stalks
sleep soundly in my studio.
Gifts of the wind that rushes round the Three Tama plains,
they're the winter's elite.
Look at the dauntless onions with straw spread beneath
    them,
dammit,
sculpture has no chance.
I'm grateful for this bunch of onions my friend gave me,
for their way of ignoring the abstract.

HARSH INSIGHT

The huge eagle, head upside down, looked at the sky.
In the sky not even leaves to scatter.
I jangled the screen.
A shudder—and
a huge eagle's dead-earnest great eyes
like a spear, swished at me.
Bristling its crest it stared at my eyes—and in turn
I stared at its eyes intently for half an hour,
work brought about by the heart's unknown pain at winter
    noon.
Eagle, I'm sorry, I said.
In this world
it's painful to see,
it's cruel to be able to see,
it's dangerous to see through.
Where on earth our solitude comes from,
this cold stone railing may know,
or this blue sky piercing through to the very end.

COMIC VERSE

As long as you've got inherited provisions stored in your
    cellar,
go ahead and look hungry,
play at being poor to be chic.
When you tire of the Parthenon and Notre-Dame,
fine, go on to lanterns, Mount Fuji,
Hiroshige, Harunobu, Bashō, Buson,
throw in Taiga, back to Sesshū,
praise the blank paper.
Pick, as you please,
tanka or haikai.
But I, who know the thing about your cellar,
won't join your playing in being chic.
You may tap me on the shoulder,
but I won't feel good.
With your wooly hands
you may tug at me
and try to seat me on the Great Road to cheap instant
    Enlightenment
but I'll have to excuse myself.
You see, like those fellows in the *Kojiki*,
I just like to shuffle about in the sun;
to tell you the truth,
—*Japon, Japon, Japon, Japon, Japon*—
ah, you're too noisy.

GRATITUDE

Thank you, France.
Understanding brightens mankind.
Even in the way a woman
poured me *café au lait* one morning,
ah, you revealed it.

THUNDER BEAST

Good, it smells of gunpowder.
Good, it trips to the thunder drum that rips the air,
drops from heaven, runs around,
scratches a flagpole
and quickly hides itself in a black cloud.
Where does the thunder beast live?
The thunder beast lives in heaven, where wind is born.
Lives in the blast echoing in the mountains.
Lives in the shell that makes a trajectory.
Lives in a fizgig.
Lives in a peony, in a willow, in pampas grass.
Lives at the tip of a young woman's eyetooth.
And, by mistake perhaps
it lives in the wrinkles on a poet's forehead.

WAITING FOR AUTUMN

I'll pour water over myself once more.
Living in a city, I begin to smell of perfumes,
climbing a mountain, I begin to smell of mists,
going to a field, I begin to smell of manure.
When I don't even like smelling of conscience,
ah I'm sticky all over.
Sun and God, keep yourselves on the other side of your orbits.
So I can wait for the day when autumn thumps in
from the southwestern corner of the sky
with my body so clean it'll knock you out,
I'll pour water over myself once more.
From ample upper arms and breasts,
rising faintly from my body all dried,
that indescribably balmy
delicious live fragrance of my own skin I'll sniff once more.

BIG SNEEZE

The gardener lets out a big sneeze.
In the third floor attic, I listen:
with 10 a.m. bright winter morning sun making
anti-frost reed screens scintillate
in the already vacant spacious garden,
a big sneeze, an echo, *clonks.*
Out of habit, he then says,
"Dammit!"
Already in his straw-sandals
he's perched on a ladder to attend a pine.
And from time to time he *clonks* a big sneeze.
It's a quiet, brilliant, clear day.

LATE NIGHT

The winter moon shines on the sheet of my bed.
It's such a quiet night.
Near Tabata a freight train belches steam.
It's the night when Toller wrote that poem.
It's the night when the Second Patriarch chopped off his arm.
It's the night when an unknown girl goes out to solicit.
It's the night when someone's mother dies.
It's the night when something fills heaven.
It's the night when I lie in bed and can't sleep.

MARS IS OUT

Mars is out.

The question, In short what should I do,
brings me back to the starting point along the path of thought
    traced with such effort.
Is it that, in short, nothing matters?
No, no, infinitely no.
Wait, and with your first strength,
destroy the weakness that hurries you to such a question.
It's base to think of a promised result.
To live for a just cause,
that alone is clean.
So as to shake up your mind further,
raise your head again
and look at that large crimson star
shining above dark quietly sleeping Komagome Heights.

Mars is out.

A cold wind rattles the seeds of honey locusts.
Dogs, fucking, run wild.
Stepping on dead leaves
I go out of the brush
onto a cliff.

Mars is out.

I do not know
what a man must do.
I do not know
what a man should try to get.
I think

that a man can be a fragment of nature.
I feel
that a man is nil and is therefore immense.
Ah, I tremble,
how reassuring that a man should be nil.
Nature which has destroyed even Nil,
how prevailing it is.

Mars is out.

Heaven turns behind me.
Innumerable distant worlds climb up.
Unlike a poet in the old days
I don't see in them angels' winking.
I hear only
something like deep waves of ether.
And the world is simply
unstoppably beautiful.
Eerie beauty filled with unknown things
presses on me.

Mars is out.

WINTER, MY FRIEND

When winter my friend clonks, sneezing,
everyone starts,
the sea tide at once is transparent.
Surely the winter, looking brusque,
winds a fox-colored mainspring
tightly into the midst of the vacant sky.
With a hoary arithmetic precision
winter pursues, persecutes the weakness of the soul,
drives it up against the wall.
Casually reading the morning paper,
I feel, at my freezing fingertips,
the winter's determination.
Last night's mental landscape
is now a crumpled mirage.
Ah, winter whips me, whips me.
Peels the skin off my face.
Makes me abandon my body.
Smashes me to bits, buries me in the snow.
Winter then says, Stand up.

I decide, All right.

WHAT'S GREAT

When Socrates died, what did he say?
A single chicken was the sudden turn of his life.
Or the wedge in his criticism of life.
If asked, Where's what's great?
I'll point to that shabby electric pole.
Weather mild for winter,
today again the chickadees will come.
Again my neighbor missy will stalk the street.
From the human weakness of thinking oneself as the center
    of Creation,
ah, someone, liberate me completely.

DAYBREAK

On the street where last night's downpour makes pebbles
    stick out,
look, already comes a young man delivering newspapers.
Good morning, I'm on my way home from an all-night
    funeral.
Walking in a spring dawn like this—
What's wrong about dying and turning into grass?

THINKING OF MOTHER

Those breasts, the heady smell in the bosom,
to which, waking at midnight, I clung.

That alley where, piggyback in the evening, I was often
    asked,
"Who do you love more, your father or your mother?"

That morning when she sent me off to school
striking flints over me because I'd hurt myself with a chisel.

That one night in Paris when I returned to my studio, drunk,
and found a letter in her crabbed handwriting waiting for
    me.

Those sunken eyes which, though I had no success or fame,
    remained trustful of me till the end,
having discarded her own hopes for life.

That small body that climbed up my stoop
and anxiously wanted to be held in my big arms.

And that unexpected, authoritative transformation
when she was about to die.

Remembering mother, I am again a fool,
the bottom falls from my life,
fears vanish.
No matter what may happen,
I feel my dead mother knows all.

15 OCCASIONAL PIECES

O

Sculpture is terrifying.
It makes what's round round.
Is what's round truly round?
Hubris gets punished.

O

In the head that's bound to die is something that doesn't.
What's bound to die, as it is,
begins to look like something that doesn't.

O

I looked at the eye and was startled:
a drop from the formless Great Void,
the alter ego of the universe,
earthly beings' link to heaven.

O

Becoming hushed,
some people give off a mountain fragrance.

O

The human body doesn't tolerate adjectives.
Arm is arm, thigh is thigh.
Adjectives vulgarize things little by little.

O

A peach is noble, auspicious,
somewhat lewd, a bit licentious;
held in the hand, it stirs.
It may possess you.

O

A great man cures his temper, it's said,
by holding two walnuts in one hand.
I hold two tempers in one hand
and smash the walnut.

O

Anger against life
can't be erased by the joy for nature.
The two are separate.
At least for the time being.

O

May what is kindly
leave my sculpture.
What is cruelly calm,
that's what I want.
Like that ginkgo trunk.

O

Until true freedom comes,
let man be angry for billions of years.
If Lao Tzu had felt no wrath,
the doctrine of do-nothing wouldn't have existed.
The Zen priest's enlightenment
must be nothing but a variation of anger.
I can't be bothered with petty anger.
I'd like to feel damn big anger.

O

A woman standing, vacant,
is prehistoric nature.
One move,
and she's back to 1927.

○

Because I don't have enough talent,
I depend on reality.
Until I see through reality,
I won't stop for a moment, I decide.

○

Carving wood, my heart grows warm.
It's as if the wood were pleased
to be taking on some form.

○

Sometimes I think:
What am I doing?
For cosmic dust
space is infinite in every direction.

○

It's good to work, adding wood in the stove,
in a studio which feels cool, mornings and evenings.
It's good to have a bit of pale smoke, as the fire starts,
leaking into the studio.
It's good to have the smell of the cigarettes my friends left
trailing like mist.
It's good, when hungry, to make cheap tea
and drink just one cup.
It would be better if there were an orchid.
It would be better still, it would be like a hermit's cave, if
        there were a woman, naked.

PEACEFUL TIME

A winter evening, I take a walk,
in the oddly lustrous silver-plate sky
a scattering of stars already appears,
on the earth a pale haze, unsettled, drifting
stagnantly as the smoke of a bluish fire,
pervades every nook of the street.
By the time electric bulbs become tinged orange,
Komagome Sendagi Hayashi-chō
becomes for a moment deserted.
At such a time
over a fence as I pass
comes a whiff of sukiyaki
and a little further, into the middle of the street
flows the smell of saury mackerels broiled with a pinch of
        salt,
from a drain nearby rises steam smelling of soap—
I come across various intimate lives.
Because, right ahead, it's an uphill slope
I'm tempted briefly to go see the town lights from the top,
        again.

TATTERED OSTRICH

What fun is there in keeping an ostrich?
Don't you see how in the twenty square yard mire of the
    zoo
its legs are too great?
How its neck is too long?
How for a country with snowfall its feathers are too tat-
    tered?
It becomes hungry, so it eats hardtack, sure,
but don't you see how the ostrich's eyes are looking only
    into the distance?
How they aren't all there, burning?
How they're waiting for an emerald wind to blow at any
    moment?
How its small innocent head is swirling with boundless
    dreams?
How it no longer is an ostrich?
Come on, people,
stop it, stop this sort of thing.

THE NATURAL THING

Because it's a natural thing
I do it, the natural thing.
Because, looking at the sky, I feel refreshed
I go out on the cliff and look at the sky.
Because, looking at the sun, I feel glad
I look through the woods at the washtub crimson daystar.
Because I become clean on the mountain
I speak with the echoes of mountain and valley.
Because, going out to the ocean, I see eternity right in front
    of me
on a ship I look at the giant constellations with surprise.
Because the flow of the river is leisurely
I stand on the coast and look without tiring.
Because thunder is a prodigious threat
I become small when it bursts.
Because a storm, clearing, leaves a fragrance
I stroll under green leaves, getting wet with raindrops.
Because a bird singing utters in its own voice something
    better than its own
I listen, fascinated, to the high twitter of a bunting on a
    cherry tree.
Because I miss my dead mother
I delight in seeing her even in a midday town.
Because women are more beautiful than flowers, and tem-
    perate
I open my heart to any woman and concentrate.
Because the human body dazzles and captivates my soul
I devour every nude there is, indulgently.
Because I don't like to mutilate people
I don't lend a hand to murder.
Because personal things are petty
I waste my life for the Way.

Because I'd like to signal everybody
I raise my hand.
Because I'd like to tell of the helter-skelter and yearnings of
my viscera
I write poetry from which only content can be picked.
Because poetry asks for living words
I respectfully keep away from borrowed clothes, however
elegant.
Because love is a subdued passion
I hope that it will fill my body like air.
Because I'm drawn by justice and beauty
I transform myself into the needle of the compass.
Because it's the natural thing
I do what I do unconcerned.

ALONE
ABSORBING OXYGEN

When people fall asleep and silent
the air at once separates into elements.

A heat-mass of poetry, like vomit,
pressures the intestines, and turns.

The eyes, kept open,
feel the bottom of the eerie, descending cold night.

Outside the window is the street,
on the street a sword of the occult.

The century shuts its mouth,
alone absorbing oxygen, poetry begins to burn in night
      heaven.

"FALLING ILL
ON A JOURNEY"

Bashō thought, lying in bed.
Haikai stood rightly, between heaven and earth.
This Way won't mislead people.
The Law of Nature won't deceive people.
The only thing I think about:
always in Nature's bosom,
I don't know where, is something that has yet to wake.
Somewhere in the crux I don't understand
is hidden the depth that pushes off these postpositives.
Who is it that calls me from the end of time that I won't see?
"Falling ill on a journey, my dreams run round a withered
    field."
I will take one step forward.

KITAJIMA SETSUZAN

Kitajima Setsuzan sleeps in mud under the bridge
because he's too fastidious to tolerate a speck of dust.

Kitajima Setsuzan does calligraphy for a grocery boy
because he knows what calligraphy is.

The April rain has changed the pressure in my ears.
Growing a little sleepy, I'm making a clay horse.

KNIFE WHETTER

Wordless, he is whetting a knife.
Sun already going, he's still whetting it.
Pressing the back blade and the front,
and changing the water, he's again whetting it.
What on earth he wants to make,
as if he did not know even that,
with split-second concentration on his brow,
he whets the knife under green leaves.
His sleeves gradually tear,
his mustache turns white.
Fury, necessity, or innocence,
or is he chasing an infinite sequence
simply, prodigiously?

THE LANKY FELLOW
KEEPS SILENT

"The stage is too far, I can't hear a thing. That old man, today is his *climax*, it would seem. The senior grade of the third rank, was it, a member of the Imperial Art Board, a professor emeritus, I hear that he doesn't have much money, but for an artisan making Buddhist images, he made it really big, didn't he? Take tonight, there are several hundred VIPs here, I guess. Celebration of his 77th year, such damn luck he has. He's fortunate too, his colleagues from those days are all dead, you know. Who are they standing behind the old man? I see, they're his sons, huh, they all look in their forties, I wonder what they do. I see, that one's doing the same old sculpture. Never heard of him. That's right, it's no good to do too many things. Jack of all trades, master of none, as they say. He must be a conceited, snotty fellow. Come to think of it, he doesn't look like his old man at all, does he? Too lanky and shabby-faced. No two masters in two generations, that says it all. Thank God, the ceremony's over, huh. Oh I see, our next entertainments are Yūki Magozaburō's puppets and old sisters' dancing, are they? Let's get closer."

"Ladies and gentlemen, dinner is served."

Packing the hall are bald heads, silverware, combed-back
    hair, *diamant*, round knots, perfumes, seven-three's,
    roses.
Nippon at nine o'clock P.M., appetites under the rococo fret-
    ted ceiling.
The steward's single finger, the service explodes.
Steams of alcohol.
Extravagantly long speech, speech, speech, speech.
Aged tears.
Banzai.

The collapse of paralyzing rituals, collapse of the ranks, collapse of goodwill, collapse of the patience shared by the organizers.

What's funny, their tails are funny. What's left, anger's left.

The lanky fellow who exposed himself determinedly to his time, keeps silent.

Stands on the street, looking at the late night Big Dipper.

Thinking about something different.

Thinking about when and how.

PORTRAIT

Respectfully I draw it.
What's before me is a single organism.
The ninety-one year old catfish is a wonder, a beauty.
The catfish smokes his gold-tipped cigarette.
"I don't mind my reputation among the people.
What worries me is the future of our nation.
That's exactly what troubles me.
Artists who do things like drawing are useless.
The portrait doesn't have to be a good likeness,
If it shows a great man, that is.
Hmm—Hmm," here his mouth expands to seven inches,
"Am I through?
You can't make Buddhist images?
That's because you don't have enough skill.
Drawing is no good.
'Full of grace and spirit' is what they say, do you know?
This morning I made a *kyōka*, which goes like this—"
Measuring this lump of avarice which is never off guard
I draw, taking care not to miss a single arc,
record the whole history, incised on the grotesque mask, of
    the capitalist development of Imperial Japan.
Ninety-one year old catfish,
don't you see what I want is the sort of cruel likeness you
    don't want?

HAUNTED HOUSE

In the square house graced with cobwebs that the master
    likes
lives the master graced with tradition, rebellion, lust for
    knowledge, and iron-fire feeling.
The master, as soon as he was born, was drilled in loyalty
    and filial piety.
The master, growing, saw all the contradictions of this
    world.
The master's insides were filled with accumulating stories
    of the floating world, which he couldn't even begin to
    touch.
The master soon held true only what he saw with his own
    eyes.
The master ignored authority and vulgarity.
The master resisted the persevering rebellions of living.
The master grew used to doing things, wordless.
The master simply lived in tactile beauty.
The master welcomed whatever came, boldly dropped every-
    thing, and let his spirit wander.
The master drove his honest fragile wife to madness.

Looking at the master raking summer grass luxuriating
    under the hedge,
neighborhood children gather.
"Yours is a haunted house, isn't it?"
"It really is."

MAKING A CARP

I make a carp.
I make a carp which sinks deep into murky water,
bears the harsh magnetic storm that clangs on his thirty-six
     scales,
perceives all, and breathes quietly.
I make the fierceness of the hushed murkiness of the carp
which, hitting the waves, leaps up a waterfall,
jumping on a cloud, turns into a dragon.
I make the silence of the carp.
The fresh leaves of June make the water green.
Delighting now in the depth of green-piling water,
the carp collects power under the murky water and doesn't
     budge.
That's the kind of carp I make.

SHARK

Open-eyed and dead, you too, scaly.
At the Ona river market your pearly belly gleams.
No matter what, your mouth is made to hold a woman's
    thigh.
Sniffing a shipwreck, you swing around,
turn upside down, and passing caressingly,
wrench off a woman's soft thigh.
Your sawlike teeth cut the bone.
You glitter with fat.
Your fins are sold to Port Canton at high prices,
your scrap meat turns into fishcake.
The one who knows the pleasure of biting off
feels a goose-flesh lust
at your mysterious fascinating hidden mouth
and stares at those for bait, clad in light kimono, clonk-
    clonking
on to the concrete fish mart in the morning.

BABOON

The caged baboon rages.
Goes blind with anger,
goes blank with fury.
Why be ashamed of his pointed nose, bristly coat,
and scarlet ass?
Shakes the cage, bites at the iron, alone, wild,
a tireless eternal hellfire.
Feeding, he curses at himself,
loving, slaughters his mate.
Trying to laugh, he roars,
trying to weep, he screams.
Trembling from blood congestion,
with the inward power that rips and bursts,
ah the baboon turns into Kharakantha Asura.
Never becomes tame,
never drops out,
always staring at the world,
he is anger, anger.

UNPRECEDENTED TIME

Unprecedented time, in silence, closes in.
Time when we bet all and live in death.
Such time is already there.
What presses close doesn't relent,
the timeless law doesn't put on a useless expression.
My business is still midway,
the world's wealth hasn't stopped starvation,
everyone eats while unable to eat,
and lives by striking at the darkness an inch ahead
when what gags itself and presses close fills the surroundings.
The skill at insect-carving no longer nourishes me,
as I ready my mind and sit alone
another year ends, the calendar is renewed.
On the streets children yell and frolic,
the winter day ruins frost mildly, warmly,
hydrangea leaves, wilted, drooping, set up a camp of ele-
      gance,
and this year too, titmice, cheeping, look in the window.
All this is beyond the human and knows no end.
So I shall meet the time quietly, strongly.
I shall put everything in order and wait serenely for the time
      to come.
I shall give all to it and become naked.
With unprecedented time closing in deliberately,
I shall wash myself in the piercing beauty of the winter sky.
I shall rise clean.

THE HISTORY OF MAKING THE STATUE OF DANJŪRŌ

Although I didn't swallow Acala's sword
I spewed a profusion of evil blood,
I became translucent as a silkworm.
The auroral luminosity in my spirit
drove me to the magnetic storm in youth's stratosphere.
I bumped into the powerful electric discharger of Meiji
    culture,
the ninth-generation Ichikawa Danjūrō.
His immense gaze shoots through the century's *Idée*,
his visceral soliloquy shakes generations of dreams,
each movement of his hand produces a precise, incompara-
    ble proportion.
Floating lightly, he is an evanescent White Heron.
Turning into a mountain, he is the powerhouse Gongorō.
This monster who incarnates the extremes of all human
    powers
in his living body
is a laconic, gentle, old man.
He fishes off Shinagawa,
eats *oden* in his garden at Chigasaki.
I was caught by what is hard to catch.
Mind lost, buried in clay, spring summer autumn winter,
trying to receive in an imaginary structure
the unstoppable wind of Meiji blowing from that small stage,
fueling my new hematogenic process,
I have reached the desperate edge of the cliff.

SITTING ALONE

A ferocious late night downpour surrounds the house.
Sitting alone in a room, desolate, without even rats,
I am holding down the carp I'm carving out of wood.
My palm touching the scales is mysteriously cold.
In the four corners around me, for no reason,
something threatening accumulates.
The carp's eyes are looking at me.
Not letting my hand go, barely breathing,
I listen to the downpour late in the summer night.
I feel as if I were in some remote land.
I begin to feel it isn't this world.

NIGHT IN THE HAUNTED HOUSE

Fatherless motherless wifeless childless.
I take my seat in the midst of cobwebs and dust,
alone, heart on fire, I open the mess kit,
eat the leftover rice gone a little sour.
Water is sweet, a night wind suggestive of autumn rises in
     the room,
my sweaty body dries.
I turn off the silly speech on the radio,
and in the depth of hushed space
millions of lives and deaths stir, oppressively,
do not cease to stir in tune with the world's involuntary
     muscles.
Are conflicts eternal abreactions?
Are fermentations necessities for future manna?
The ferocious way in which what must come, comes,
one can't get angry at others.
From somewhere the smell of a racial war soon to come.
It's like the smell of cresol.
I stand in front of the mirror.
What's there is an *ocre-jaune* nude body.

CARVING A CICADA

I sit by the window full of winter sun and carve a cicada.
Dry, withered, light on my palm, the cicada
severed from the baseness of living,
even its mouth for food doesn't know it exists.
The cicada sits on a corner of the Tempyō desk.
I look at its wings.
Brittle, thin, transparent fragments of heaven,
the immaterial wings of this insect
slowly avalanche without threatening
and lightly enclose the black-and-green-adorned armor.
From the skin of the cypress I carve,
a wood fragrance rises and fills the room.
I forget time and place, I forget the age,
I forget people, I forget breathing.
The workplace I call four-and-a-half mats
seems afloat somewhere in heaven.

SETTING SUN

The equinox close, evening clearing, in the western sky the
    sun sets.
A molten, burning, red globe of iron,
even while I watch, plunges to the bottom of the woods.
Between here and there, 90 million miles apart,
what an exchange of extravagant speeds.
I throw off the sheets I was making the bed with,
put my elbows on the second floor windowsill, and watch.
Years and months fly now, before my eyes.
People grow old in quantities, and die in quantities,
but the link to timelessness comes from those speeds.
Within my blink is eternity.
Behind the life-mechanisms of this earth
man has swift and quiet heaven.
In fading zodiacal light Mercury inclines,
gigantic Venus and Jupiter, shoulder to shoulder,
thunder through boundless time and space.

LIVING AND COOKING BY MYSELF

I have yet to do anything that deserves praise.
I don't have the slightest idea of such things.
I have no father, no mother, no wife, no child,
I have wood chips, clay, waste paper, dust.
I pluck grass leaves and put them in a pot,
I stretch out the rationed rice that I eat.
In my kitchen Rikyū makes fire,
in my study Rinzai is seated,
in my studio the Creator's work is slow and leisurely.
Sixty years is neither a dream nor a phenomenon,
as I touch them, the years and months go away
and ordinary mornings and evenings come.
One, two, three, four, five, six, says a monk.

BEAUTIFUL DEAD LEAF

In front of a police box I picked up a dead leaf.
A large dead leaf of a plane tree.
By its stem I hold it against the sun:
half gold, half verdigris
dye this slightly crinkled feather fan.
I like dead leaves of any kind.
Always abundant and warm,
rustling, never cloying,
they fly off if wind blows,
and before you know it, again pile up all around
and are bathing in autumn sun.
The smell of dead leaves is the smell of your native land,
above all, how friendly the blue smoke of burning leaves.
Ah, how graceful those people of old
who kindled crimson leaves in the woods and heated their
    wine.
Although there's no wine to heat now,
friend, burn the dead leaves piled mountainously in your
    garden
and obtain potash for the farm behind your house.
I'm thinking how I should carve in wood
this leaf of a plane tree that I have picked.

TO GENERAL KURIBAYASHI

From his camp in the mainland's last outpost, Iwo Jima,
General Kuribayashi wired his last message.
Its words, cutting, do not allow mere perusal;
I read, chewing each word,
and reach the end, three tanka.
The 31-syllable lines rend my ears.
The Empire's marrow general, pushed to the wall,
bullets exhausted, out of water,
leads his remaining troops in the final charge.
First, he speaks a few words,
and the words spit blood.
Still, they're serene, the sounds correct,
the thought respectful and of all ages.
Intent on the road ahead of the Empire,
he's determined to be reborn seven times, to take the spear,
to become a fence for the Sovereign.
General Kuribayashi is still on the island.
Living in tens of thousands of deaths,
we too shall simply, simply, smash up the enemy.

THE SNOW HAS
PILED WHITE

The snow has piled white.
The snow has buried the wood path evenly.
Stepping on it, I sink to my knees and deeper;
the snow, bathed in twilight, phosphorescent,
gleams blue, resembling a sea-fire.
Crossing the path, dots, a rabbit's footprints, trail
and the depths of pine woods faintly blur.
I walk ten steps and rest to breathe.
I walk twenty steps and sit in the snow.
There's no wind, but the snow soughs from treetop to tree-
      top,
the entire spectacle incites poetry.
Mount Hayachine already crystallizes at the cloudline,
but my poetry has yet to acquire definite edges.
I pick dead cedar leaves
to heat a bowl of porridge at the hearth this evening.
Defeated, I feel evened,
something like phosphorescence glistens in my soul and is
      beautiful.
Beautiful and finally difficult to capture.

HUNGER FOR
THE HUMAN BODY

The sculptor is starved on the mountain.
There's plenty to eat on the mountain,
but no feast of bodies,
no delicacy of nudes.
Spirit protein-starved.
Hungry ghost of sculpture.
Here goes the snow again.

The thirst stabs his chest.
He bites on ice, complains to the dark night sky.
Snow Woman, come out.
Eat up this sculptor.
When you eat him, dance on this snow field.
Then the sculptor would make out of snow
your pliant body,
its two flexible protuberances
its shaded cave-in
and the smooth region and bulging portions on its back.

The spine evolves
into the skull, into the pelvis.
The promontories on the left and right become arms and legs.
Tendons manipulate, flesh mobilizes,
skin conceals everything
and delicately exposes everything.
Sculpture doesn't eat this lump of flesh.
It takes it apart into pieces
and assembles the pieces into an advanced body.
But the sculptor, for his appetite,
first devours it raw.

Great calculation of the astronomical mechanism
is the work of the truculent energy that occurs.
Intellect then is merely a chain of precision compasses.

Snow Woman doesn't show up.
Snow storms and shakes the hut,
snowflakes hit the sculptor's cheeks at will.
He sits alone by the hearth, makes a big fire,
bears the threat, the hunger for the human body.
The threat fills heaven and earth.
In the clear sky lies a white cloud, the Countess,
the barks of beech trees are powerful *gigots* exposed,
rocks have sex distinctions,
mountains are all giant torsos.
Benvenuto saw salamanders in the fire.
This sculptor sees nudes in blazing flames.

The war robbed him of everything.
The place to work, the materials for sculpture,
every structure was reduced to ashes.
With the set of chisels that he protected at risk of his life
he put himself on a mountain of Iwate.
To what fate his fate leads
no one knows.
The world doesn't know the meaning of the negative num-
        bers
that time lets out of the sculptor's hands.
He contemplates alone, quietly,
and acknowledges with good grace it's historically natural
this can't be the cinquecento.
Nippon still can't have a modern portrait.
As long as the mountain of Iwate is poor,
nothing can be done about reality.
That *Commandant* has an unusually sculpturesque head,
but this sculptor will end up having nothing to do with it.
Other contemporary sculptors

will be reduced to nothing and vanish.
On the mountain the sculptor is starved for the human body,
tonight too, his spirit roams in illusions and dreams
and finally becomes drunk, comfortably buried
in dense history and the snow,

HANDS WET WITH MOON

Since my hands are heavy
they don't turn easily.
Turn them over, and it may rain
but they aren't afraid of rain.
The moon shines on mountain pampas grass,
tonight too, chestnuts insistently fall.
Chestnuts explode by themselves and fall,
and their sound quietly pierces heaven and earth.
I don't call the moon the Lunar God.
The watery moonlight
comes over miles from a dead volcanic mass.
Things as they are, are all beautiful
and need no intermediary thought.
Beauty is one with things,
heart lives simply in sculpture.
Again a fox crosses the field.
The mid-autumn moon, bright and small, culminates.
Once more I look at my hands
wet with moon.

PART II
CHIEKO

TO SOMEONE

No, no, I don't like it
your going away—

Like fruit coming before blossom
like bud sprouting before seed
like spring immediately following summer,
that's not logical, please don't do
so unnatural a thing.
A husband as if cast in a mold
and you with your smooth round handwriting,
the mere thought makes me cry.
You, who are timid as a bird,
willful as a gale,
you are to be a bride

No, no, I don't like it
your going away—

How can you so easily,
how shall I say, as it were
put yourself on sale?
Because you *are* putting yourself on sale.
From the world of one person
to the world of millions,
and yielding to a man,
yielding to nonsense,
what an ugly thing to do.
It's like a Titian
set out for shoppers in Tsurumaki-chō.
I am lonely, sad.
Though I really don't know what to do,
it's just like watching

the large gloxinia you gave me rot,
like watching it leave me and rot,
like seeing a bird fly off into the sky
not knowing where to,
it's the sad abandon of a wave as it shatters,
brittle, lonely, searing
—But it isn't love
Mother of God
No, it isn't, it isn't.
I don't know what it is
but I don't like it
your going away—
you're going away to be a bride,
offering yourself to the will of a man you don't even know

FEAR

No, you must not
touch this quiet water,
much less throw a stone in it.
Even the tremor of a drop
wastes thousands of wave-motions.
You must respect the water's quiet
and weigh the value of quietude.

You must not say any more.
What you are about to say is one of the greatest dangers on
      earth.
If you keep your mouth shut, it'll be all right.
Open up, and it'll be lightning and fire.
You're a woman.
They say you're like a man, but after all you're a woman.
You are that round moon perspiring in the dark blue sky,
a moon that would lead the world to a dream, replace a
      moment with eternity.
That's good, that's good.
You must not turn the dream back to reality,
swing eternity back to a moment.
And you must not throw such a dangerous thing
into this clear water.

The quietude of my heart is a treasure I bought with blood,
a treasure for which I have sacrificed blood that you would
      not understand.
This quietude is my life,
this quietude is my god,
and an exacting god,
who, on a summer night, even for food,

would swirl up a fiercer disturbance.
Are you going to touch that spot?

No, you must not.
You must weigh the value of quietude.
Or else
you must get to it with an unusual resolve.
The wave-motions caused by that single stone
might fall upon you and engulf you,
might give you a blow a hundred times harder.
You're a woman.
You must become strong enough to withstand it.
Can you do it?
You must not say any more.
No, you must not.

Look,
doesn't that sooty, greasy station
in this moonlight, this sultry haze,
look like a treasure house enveloping some great beauty?
The lights of those green and red signals
play a great role between silence and parting
attuning themselves to the moonlit night in the distance.
Now I'm surrounded with something,
with a certain atmosphere,
with a certain formless power of mysterious adjustment,
I'm holding on to a valuable equilibrium.
My soul thinks of eternity,
my naked eyes see an infinite value in all things.
Be still, be still.
I'm continually touching a certain power,
oblivious of words.

No, you must not
touch this quiet water,
much less throw a stone in it.

TO SOMEONE
IN THE SUBURBS

My heart, now like a great wind, sweeps toward you,
my love.
Now seeping into the blue fish skin the cold night grows late,
sleep peacefully in your house in the suburbs.
An infant's truthfulness is all that is you.
So clear and transparent
anyone looking at it discards his evil intent,
and good and evil, without disguise, appear before it.
You are indeed a supreme judge.
In the various soiled figures that I'd become,
with infant truthfulness
you found my noble self.
What you found is strange to me
but, because I consider you a supreme judge,
relying on you I rejoice in my heart
and believe that what is hidden in my warm flesh
is the self that I do not know.
It is winter, the zelkovas leaves have all fallen.
Tonight there is not a sound.
My heart, now like a great wind, sweeps toward you.
It is a noble tender spring that wells out of the depths of the
        earth
and wets your clear skin, neglecting not a corner.
My heart leaps, dances, flaps about
exactly as you move,
but never forgets to protect you,
my love.
This is an incomparable fountain of life.
So sleep you, peacefully.
Because this is a cold winter night like a felon,
for now sleep peacefully in your house in the suburbs,
sleep like an infant.

TO SOMEONE

Not as a game
not to kill time
you come to see me
—not painting, not reading, not working—
and for two days, for three days
we laugh, lark, frolic, and make love
compress time at will
spend several days in a second

Ah, and yet
it's not a game
not to kill time
for our overflowing selves it's the only life
the only living
and the only power.
The wealth of nature in August
which seems too wasteful, far too excessive,
those grasses that bloom and decay deep in mountains
sunlight that cries out
throngs of clouds moving infinitely
overabundant thunderbolts
rain and water
green, red, blue, and yellow
those forces that spout out into the world
how can we possibly say they are wasted?
You dance for me
I sing for you,
walk every second of life fully.
At the moment of tossing a book
at the moment of opening a book
I amount to the same.
Empty diligence

and empty indolence
shouldn't be associated with me.
When your loving heart bursts
you come to see me
discarding all, overcoming all
trampling upon all
and joyfully

LATE NIGHT SNOW

The warm fire in the fireplace
makes a faint noise.
The light in the closed-in study
quietly shines on the two of us, a little tired.
The evening clouds have turned to snow.
Looking out a while ago
we saw white all around.
The snow that goes on piling up noiselessly
weighs on the ground, the roofs, and on our hearts,
a soft weight enfolding pleasures.
The world holds its breath, wide-eyed, like a child.
"Look, already so much snow!"
a smudged voice in the distance
and soon, the clop-clop of someone kicking the snow off his
        clogs.
Then silence, no words, and as it turns eleven,
nothing more to talk about,
tea somewhat numbing,
we hold hands,
listen to the deep heart of this voiceless world,
contemplate the flow of time
and, slightly perspiring, full of peace,
we feel ready to accept all the emotions there are, of any-
        one's.
Again, the clop-clop-clop, kicking the snow off,
then the rumble of a car—
"Come, look at the snow!"
I say, and the one who responds
suddenly begins to live a fairy tale,
opens her mouth a little,
delighting at the snow.

The snow too delights at the night
and goes on piling in innumerable flakes,
warm snow, the heavy snow
closing in on our bodies—

FOUNTAIN OF MANKIND

The world has turned a youthful green,
and blue rain falls again.
Its sound,
manifesting a swarm of stirring organisms,
always terrifies me.
And my aroused soul
goes over me, gets away from me
and goes on and on making me.
Now it dies, now it's born.
As two o'clock becomes three
and further from a green leaf sprouts another young leaf,
today too I've been feeling this acceleration
fill my breast.
And in an extreme quietude
I've been sitting still.
Tears falling,
I've been thinking intensely of you, as if holding you.
You are truly the other half of me.
You must assuredly hold my trust,
you deeply share the rigor of my flesh.
For me, there is you,
there is you.
I have tasted human solitude cruelly.
You know I have plunged into the terrible realm of self-
      abandonment.
You alone
are kind enough to see my life from its roots,
understand me as a whole.
I am the pioneer of the road I take.
I am right as grass and trees are right.
Ah, you are kind enough to see it with your own eyes.
Surely you have your own life.

You have the fluid power of sea water.
That for me there is you
means that for me there is a smile.
Because of you my life becomes complex, becomes rich.
And knowing solitude, I don't feel solitude.
In the society in which I live
I have already taken several steps onto my road from the
    path that thousands pass on.
There are no longer friends with whom I do things.
There are only friends with whom I share partial understand-
    ing.
I have come not to be saddened by this solitude.
Because it is natural, and it is inevitable.
And I even try to be content with this solitude.
Yet
if for me there were not you—
ah, I cannot even imagine it,
it's foolish even to imagine it.
For me, there is you,
there is you.
And in you, there is a large world of love.
Though I have gone away from people to solitude,
through you I contact the live breath of mankind again,
become active in humanity.
Ridding myself of everything
I simply go toward you
to immerse myself in a deep, distant fountain of mankind.
You were born for me.
For me, there is you,
there is you, there is you.

IN ADORATION OF LOVE

Body's desire that knows no end
the terrible power of a rising tide—
in the fire that flares up still more, perspiring,
salamanders twist and turn, dancing.

The ceaseless snow throws a feast of *vol nuptial* late at night
and shouts out joy in the hushed air.
Shattered by beauty and power
we then immerse ourselves in an esoteric flow
breathe in an aroused rosy haze
and reflected on the jewels in Indra's net
mold our lives inexhaustibly.

The cradling demon's power that lurks in winter
and the raw heat of sprouts that bud in winter—
what burns inside everything pulsates with time
and lets electric currents of ecstasy echo through our bodies.

Our skins wake ferociously
our bowels thrash about in the glee of existence
hair becomes phosphorescent
fingers acquire their own lives and crawl clinging all over
        the bodies
the world of chaos, of sincerity, that stores the word
swiftly reveals itself above us.

Full of light
full of happiness
all discriminations circle a single sound
poison and manna share a box
unbearable pain convolves our bodies
supreme rapture illuminates the mystery, the labyrinth.

Buried warm under the snow
we melt in natural elements
feed on endless earthly love
and praise our life, in the distance.

DINNER

Go out in gust-thrashed downpour
like a drowned rat
buy three pints of rice
for 24 *sen* and 5 *rin*
five dried fish
one pickled radish
red ginger
eggs from the chicken coop
seaweed hard as beaten steel
fried dumplings
salted bonito guts

Heat some water
eat like hunger-devils: our dinner

The storm builds
slams against the roof-tiles
shakes, rattles the house.
Our appetite holds out sturdily,
food turns into blood, urges the instinct.
Soon, surfeited, blissful
we hold hands quietly
cry unlimited joy in our hearts
and pray:
may the daily trivia have life
may life's every detail be illuminated
may each of us overflow
may we always be full

Our dinner acquires
a power fiercer than the storm.
Eating done, satiety

awakens in us a mysterious lust
makes us marvel at our limbs
and burn in the violent rain

This is dinner for poor people like us

TWO UNDER THE TREE

Far down the road, two pine trees in
the Adachi field—under the pine
trees I see someone standing

That's Mount Atatara,
that glistening is Abukuma river.

Sitting like this, with few words,
I feel through my head half lulled to sleep
only the pine wind of distant times blowing light green.
In this large landscape in early winter
I burn quietly, holding your hand—let me not hide my joy
from that white cloud looking down.

Myrrh rising ever from your soul
oh into what depths of love you draw me.
The perspective of the ten years, seasons we've walked
    together,
reveals in you only the infinity of woman.
What smolders in that infinity is precisely
what cleanses me of desires,
what pours youth into my troubled life.
Elusive as a demon, it keeps
oddly changing, doesn't it?

That's Mount Atatara,
that glistening is Abukuma river.

This is where you were born,
those tiny white dots are your family wine cellars.
Now let me stretch out my legs
and under this vacant cloudless northern sky

enjoy the air fragrant with trees.
Let me wash my body in this atmosphere like you,
cool, pleasant, curving, pliant.
Tomorrow I must leave, go
to the city of infamy, the chaotic maelstrom of love and hate,
into the midst of human comedy
that I dread and yet cling to.
This is where you were born,
the heaven and earth that gave birth to your mysterious
    unique flesh.
The pine wind is still blowing.
Tell me once more about the geography of this panorama,
    of this desolate land in early winter.

That's Mount Atatara,
that glistening is Abukuma river.

CATTLE ON A MAD RUN

Ah, you are so frightened because
you saw what just passed.
Like a specter,
thundering through those black pines,
an avalanche in this zone of deep silence,
now completely gone,
that cattle herd on a mad run.

Let's call it a day,
the triangular ridge of Hotaka we were painting
is covered with terre-verte clouds.
The cerulean Azusa river
that carries melted snow down Yari
is overwhelmed by the mountains.
Far away, the valley aspens stream in the wind.
Let's stop painting for today
and make a fire, as usual,
small enough not to defile this gods' garden, long untouched
        by humans.
Here, on the moss nature has swept clean,
come, sit down quietly.

You are so frightened because you saw,
chasing the cows in their wild stampede,
that terrible, breathless,
bloody, young, transfigured bull.
But someday you will pity the naked bestiality
you saw on this divine mountain,
someday when your body has known more,
smiling with quiet love—

CATFISH

There's a leap, a splash in the pail.
As night deepens the knife-blade grows lucid.
Woodcarving is the job of the north wind of winter night.
Even if we run out of coal for the fire place,
catfish,
would you rather feed on vast dreams under the ice?
The cypress chips are my family,
Chieko is not alarmed at our poverty.
Catfish,
your fins have swords,
your tail has antennae,
your gills have blackgold trimmings,
your optimism such a blockhead—
what interesting greetings to my work!
The wind falls, on the wood floor there's a smell of orchid.
Chieko has gone to sleep.
I push aside the half-carved catfish,
change the water for the whetstone
and for tomorrow's sharpness confidently whet my knife.

TWO AT NIGHT

That we will end up starving
the gelid night rain prophesied, falling wetly on snow.
Chieko is a woman of uncommon resolution,
but still she treasures a medieval dream, preferring death by
  fire to starvation.
Grown wholly silent we once again listen to the rain.
The wind seems to have risen slightly, rose branches claw
  against the windowpane.

CHILD'S TALK

Chieko says Tokyo has no sky at all,
says she wants to see the real sky.
Surprised, I look at the sky:
there among fresh cherry leaves
is a familiar, clear sky
that I can't separate from.
The dull, smoldering haze at the horizon
is the pink moist of the morning.
Looking far off Chieko says:
The blue sky that every day comes out
above Mount Atatara is
the real sky I mean.
This is just child's talk of the sky.

LIFE IN PERSPECTIVE

A bird flaps up from your feet.
Your wife goes insane.
Your clothes turn to rags.
Range: ten thousand feet.
Ah this gun is too long.

CHIEKO RIDING THE WIND

Chieko, now mad, will not speak
and only with blue magpies and plovers exchanges signs.
Along the hill-range of windbreaks
pine pollen flows everywhere yellow and
in the wind of clear May, Kujūkuri Beach grows hazy.
Chieko's robe appears and disappears among the pines,
on the white sands there are truffles growing.
Gathering them, I
slowly follow after Chieko.
The blue magpies and plovers now are her friends.
To Chieko who has already given up being human
this terrifyingly beautiful morning sky is the finest place to
        walk.
Chieko flies.

CHIEKO PLAYING
WITH PLOVERS

Where there is no one on the sands of Kujūkuri
sitting on the sand Chieko plays alone.
Innumerable friends call to Chieko.
Chii, chii, chii, chii, chii—
Leaving tiny footprints on the sand,
plovers come near her.
Chieko who is always talking to herself
raises both hands to call them.
Chii, chii, chii—
Plovers beg for the shells in her hands.
Chieko scatters them here and there.
Rising up in a flock the plovers call Chieko.
Chii, chii, chii, chii, chii—
Leaving off entirely the task of being human,
now having passed into the natural world
Chieko seems just a speck.
Some two hundred yards off in the windbreak, in the eve-
        ning sun
bathed in pine pollen I stand, forgetting time.

INVALUABLE CHIEKO

Chieko sees what one cannot see,
hears what one cannot hear.

Chieko goes where one cannot go,
does what one cannot do.

Chieko does not see the living me,
yearns for the me behind me.

Chieko has cast off the weight of suffering,
has strayed out to the endless, desolate zone of beauty.

I persistently hear her call to me, but
Chieko no longer has a ticket to the human world.

TWO AT THE FOOT
OF THE MOUNTAIN

The back mountain of Bandai that splits in two and leans
stares fiercely at the August sky above.
Its skirts spread out, trail into the distance
and a profusion of pampas grass overwhelms.
Half mad, my wife sits with the grass beneath her
and leaning heavily on my arm
like a small girl cries without ceasing
—I'll go to pieces pretty soon—
Borne away by the demon of fate that assaults consciousness
she takes inevitable leave of her soul.
Premonition of the inexorable
—I'll go to pieces pretty soon—
The mountain wind feels cold to my hands wet with tears.
Wordless, I look intently at the figure of my wife.
Turning to me once more at the border of awareness
she clings to me.
Now there is not in the world a means to recover her.
My heart in this moment splits, drops away
and in the sharp silence becomes one with the universe that
    wraps us two.

LEMON ELEGY

So intensely you had been waiting for lemon.
In the sad, white, light deathbed
you took that one lemon from my hand
and bit it sharply with your bright teeth.
A fragrance rose the color of topaz.
Those heavenly drops of juice
flashed you back to sanity.
Your eyes, blue and transparent, slightly smiled.
You grasped my hand, how vigorous you were.
There was a storm in your throat
but just at the end
Chieko found Chieko again,
all life's love into one moment fallen.
And then once
as once you did on a mountain top you let out a great sigh
and with it your engine stopped.
By the cherry blossoms in front of your photograph
today, too, I will put a cool fresh lemon.

TO ONE WHO DIED

The sparrows wake at daybreak as you used to and tap on
 my window.
The gloxinias near my pillow bloom silently as you used to.

The morning wind, as though it were human, wakens my
 limbs,
your fragrance is cool in my bedroom at five a.m.

Casting off the white sheets, I stretch my arms,
and welcome your smile in the summer morning sun.

You whisper to me what today is.
You stand like someone with authority.

I become your child,
you become my fresh young mother.

You are here, you're still here.
You become everything and fill me.

Though I don't think I deserve your love,
your love ignores all and envelops me.

PLUM WINE

The bottle of plum wine that Chieko who died had made,
murky and stagnant with the weight of ten years and con-
cealing the light,
now amber in a cup, thickened, looks like a gem.
I think of the person who left it, saying,
"Have some of this
when you're alone and cold, late at night in early spring."
Threatened by the anxiety that her head was going to be
destroyed,
sorrowed by the thought that she was going to pieces pretty
soon,
Chieko put her things in order.
Seven years' madness ended in death.
I savor quietly, quietly
the fragrant sweetness of the plum wine I found in the
kitchen.
Even the screams of the world in madness and stress
can't touch this second.
Looking this pitiful instance of life straight in the eye,
the world can only step back.
The night wind has stopped.

BARREN HOMECOMING

Chieko, so anxious to return,
has come home dead.
Late in the October night, I sweep
a small corner of the empty studio
and put there Chieko, carefully.
Before this single human body that does not move
I stand, lost.
People set the screens upside down.
People light candles, burn incense.
People make up Chieko's face.
And so things get done by themselves.
Day breaks, night comes,
all around there's noise and gaiety,
the house fills with flowers,
it comes to look like someone else's funeral,
and before I know it, Chieko is gone.
In the deserted, dark studio I stand alone.
Outside, there's a full moon, or so they say.

SHŌAN TEMPLE

At Shōanji, an old temple of the Jōdo sect,
in the rustic town called Hanamaki, Ōshū,
on the anniversary of your death, in recurring autumn
  showers,
I had a truly modest service for you.
The town of Hanamaki was also bombed
and the Shōanji, completely burnt,
was a shed, a two-mat place
with an altar in it.
The rain blew in through the papered doors behind me,
wetting the skirt of the priest's robe.
The priest read the One Page on Salvation
as prescribed, in a quiet voice, feelingly.
The terrifying truth of the confession of someone in the
  ancient past
who cast himself out, believing in the Buddha,
struck me, living now, as very much alive.
In front of the Buddha in the shed-altar of Shōanji
I again remembered intensely
the procession of your life, which, your trust boundless,
burned up for me.

DREAM

By that smart mountain cable car with Chieko
I went to peer into the crater of Vesuvius.
The apparent dream was as corpuscular as spice,
Chieko wrapped me in the mist of her twenties.
At the tip of the slender bamboo-like telescope
burning gas spurted as from a jet plane.
Through the telescope Mount Fuji appeared.
At the bowl's base there seemed to be something interesting,
on the bowl's surrounding stands there were many people.
At the foot of Mount Fuji Chieko had made a sheaf of seven
        autumn grasses
and threw it deep into the crater of Vesuvius.
Chieko was warm, beautiful, pure,
yet full of endless infatuation.
That female body burning translucent as mountain water,
she walked leaning on me, treading the crumbling sands.
All around, the Pompeian stench was suffocating.
The inharmony of my whole being until yesterday vanished
and in the autumn-fresh mountain hut at 5 a.m. I woke.

METROPOLIS

Into the depth of nature that Chieko longed for
the turning of fate has cast me.
Fate destroyed the living Chieko in the capital
and put me, a child of the capital, here.
The mountains of Iwate are rough, beautiful, immaculate,
they surround me, they are merciless.
Hypocrisy and idleness cannot exist in this soil.
I hurry like nature breathlessly
and advance, throwing my naked body ahead.
Chieko who died lives again,
lives here, lodged in my flesh
and delights in being soiled with river, mountain, grass, tree.
Phenomena of a cosmos endlessly transforming,
rising and falling of generations that forever turn,
all these Chieko receives
and I touch them as well.
My heart goes merry,
sitting by the fireplace of my small hut
which others say is solitary living in the mountains,
alone, I think this is the metropolis on earth.

SOLILOQUY ON A NIGHT OF BLIZZARD

Outside, there's a blizzard raging.
On a night like this the rats stay put,
the village is far off, hushed into sleep,
there's no other soul on the mountain.
I throw a big stump on the fire,
it burns splendidly.
My physiology sixty-seven years old,
I think I feel much easier now.
As long as lust is there,
I tell you, doing real work is hard.
The work called art, at its depths,
demands such inhumanity.
Total absence of lust of course wouldn't help.
Better say, I've known it thoroughly and now don't have it.
If Chieko appeared here now
she'd simply be all gaiety, and laugh.
What comes out of this harsh inhumanity,
a barely perceptible fragrance, is perhaps
what they call god's rhyme.
Though senility wouldn't be too good.

PART III
A BRIEF HISTORY
OF IMBECILITY

FAMILY

KOWTOW
(Promulgation of the Constitution)

I was on someone's back.
The hill of Ueno was crammed with people;
over their heads I saw,
along the center of the snowy road cleared of people,
two files of cavalrymen coming.
Someone, with me still on his back,
pried open the wave of people and forced himself out to the
    front.
I was put down.
Everybody was to kowtow.
The hoofs of the mounted policemen's horses
kicked the snow in front of my head.
Several closed carriages passed,
and after a little interval
I saw cavalrymen with Imperial standards held erect,
and in the carriage that followed
I saw two persons.
At that moment my head was shoved down hard
by someone's hand.
I smelled pebbles wet with snow.
"You'd go blind."

TOPKNOT

Grandfather had his topknot cut off.
" 'You ol' fogey's' all they say,
but I didn't want my topknot cut off, to tell the truth.
Katsu, that damn barber, tells me
the Mikado says
'Get a crew cut for civilization and enlightenment.'
No matter what the officials and the cops say to me,
I don't twitch a muscle,
but if that's what the Mikado says,
I can't win.
The shogun is the head clerk,
the Mikado is the boss.
And the word's from *him*, right?
I was so mad,
that cursed topknot Katsu cut like a treasure,
I didn't even bring it home."

FIRST LIEUTENANT GUNJI

The story of First Lieutenant Gunji's National Duty Society
Mr. Katō told us in the classroom.
It was the story of several boats that started from the Sumida
    river
and only a few days before had been shipwrecked off Mount
    Kinka.
How the tragic attempt to go by boat to the end of Chishima
had come about
Mr. Katō told us, in tears.
The pupils listened, all in tears.
That a graduate of Shitaya
was among the shipwrecked
excited the pupils of Shitaya.
How noble it is
to sacrifice oneself,
our teacher explained afterward to us earnestly.
All of us listened, our hopes high.

SINO-JAPANESE WAR

Grandfather piled his fists
on top of his nose.
"He's got to be Mr. T."
It was the story of Harada Jūkichi breaking the Turtle Gate.
"Mr. T. on the Kobu plains
goes to and fro, night and day.
All for the Mikado.
Think of it, Mitsu."
Whenever night came,
I pricked my ears and trembled.
Surely there was some noise on the roof.
Wings beating, that is.

SCULPTING IN
THE IMPERIAL PRESENCE

Father, unusually tense,
cleaned his workshop and carved wood for seals.
In an instant he finished and showed the result to everyone,
including me, a child.
On the splendid stem of cherry wood
was a deer carved with a single knife.
His society was going to have an Imperial visit the next day,
and he was ordered to sculpt in the Imperial presence, father
    said.
The carving was a rehearsal.
Father took a bath, purified his body,
and the next day had flints sparked on himself and left home.
He's going to show it to the Emperor, in person.
So fortunate for him.
"May he be free from any mistakes,"
mother said, and prayed at the Buddhist altar.
A child, I was much agitated
that he didn't come home though the sun had set.
At the rickshawman's cry, "He's home,"
I flew to the front door.

FUNDS FOR
BUILDING WARSHIPS

The Sino-Japanese War was over
but war consciousness rose still higher.
To be prepared for the next war
funds for building warships had to be scraped together.
First, His Majesty gave a large sum,
and government officials were to have part of their salaries
    deducted
for some years to come.
Father told mother and me about it in detail
at night in the dining room.
The return of the Liaotung Peninsula,
the Emperor was terribly worried,
father feared from the bottom of his heart.
"So from now on, Mitsu, don't be wasteful.
Understand?"

THE STATUE
OF LORD KUSUNOKI

"Nothing went wrong."
That was all father said.
His Majesty's wish to see
the wooden model of Lord Kusunoki's statue was conveyed
and the School of Arts was in an uproar.
Preparations were made in the greatest detail,
the wooden model was taken apart, transported,
and assembled again inside the Double Bridge.
Father was the supervisor.
His Majesty came out briskly into the garden
and walked around the wooden model.
Because a single pin was missing
from a sword-shaped antler on the helmet,
the antler swayed each time there was a wind.
If it fell, he would disembowel himself—
that was father's determination, I was told afterward.
In front of the hibachi in the dining room
he didn't talk much—his face showed
not only a gladness of relief
but something rueful as well
because the narrow escape was still with him.
He had been ready to die.
Unknown to anyone, afterward I shed tears.

MODULATION

SCULPTURE ONLY

The first nibble in Japan's expansion tragedy,
the Russo-Japanese War, was remote to me.
Only the dire story of Port Arthur,
the extra on the Japan Sea battle,
and the sharp contrast between Ambassador Komura and
    Count Witte
were impressed in my memory.
Passing my twentieth year I stayed on at graduate school,
I was absorbed night and day
in training in sculpture.
Utterly ignorant of the world, heaven and earth inside a jar,
I wanted only to grasp the truth of sculpture.
Both father and the other teachers at school appeared to be
    no more than artisans.
I wanted to know more than an artisan would.
In dark surroundings, groping,
I searched for the sculpture of the world.
I don't remember when,
but Takuboku, who came intending to talk to me,
**finding a spoiled child interested only in sculpture, who
    ignored the world,**
gave up and went home.
I wanted to know more about a man called *Rojin*
than the outcome of the Russo-Japanese War.

PARIS

I became an adult in Paris.
It was in Paris that I first knew the other sex.
It was in Paris that I first had my soul liberated.
Paris accomodated any species of mankind
as a matter of course.
It doesn't refuse any lineage of thinking.
It doesn't wither any heterogeneity of beauty.
Be it good or bad, new or old, high or low,
it lets whatever is in human categories co-habit
and leaves the rest to the inevitable self-cleansing process.
The charms of Paris grasp you.
You can breathe in Paris.
Modernity originates in Paris,
beauty becomes ready and sprouts,
new brain cells are born in Paris.
Living in a corner of this bottomless world capital
where France exists transcending France,
I forgot, at times, my nationality.
My native land was remote, small, petty,
it was like some bothersome village.
I was first enlightened to sculpture in Paris,
had my eyes opened to the truth of poetry,
and recognized the reasons for culture
in each citizen there.
Saddened and helpless,
I saw an unmatchable gap.
I felt nostalgic for, yet denied,
everything Japanese, the way the country was.

REBELLION

UNFILIAL

Kobe looked like a narrow, close cage.
Fujiyama was beautiful but small.
With my overjoyed father and mother before me
I apologized in my heart.
They didn't know what was in the head of a man
once said to be so considerate to his parents.
For me to become unfilial
couldn't be helped, in the name of humanity.
I was going to live as an individual.
That simply meant rebellion
in this country where nothing tolerated human beings.
The dream of a home for which father and mother had been
        happily waiting
would be broken first.
What was going to happen,
I didn't know myself.
That I'd deviate from good manners and pretty customs was
        the only sure thing.
"Look at his face, sleeping,"
mother whispered by my pillow.
What was I going to do with this kind of loving kindness
        now?

DECADENCE

Sculpture oil painting poetry prose,
the more I did it the more I sponged.
No to a campaign for bronze statues.
No to teaching school.
No to marriage and courtship offers.
Then what can we do?
He's such a pain in the neck,
that's what all your relatives are saying about you.
Sipping liqueur at Stork's Nest at the Yoroi Bridge,
I was drunk, feigning devil-may-care indifference.
I was drinking as if drunk.
I had absolutely no way to go.
People were amused, saying, "He's *decadent*,"
but I hadn't known such a painful waking of conscience.
Belatedly came my youth,
I fell deeper into the depths.
Perfectly conscious, I slipped down.
Had I had anything to do with Catholicism
I would have turned to the Cross.
It was not the Cross, but Chieko,
that appeared before me, a scapegrace, like a miracle.

HOLING UP

LIVING IN BEAUTY

Purified by a woman's love
I finally gained my self.
Continuing indescribable poverty
I plunged once again into the world of beauty.
My innate tendency to segregate myself
made me concentrate on forging my individuality,
made me feel remote from the world's conflicts.
Politics, economy, and even social movements
appeared to be no more than shadows.
The two of us, Chieko and I,
fighting for a life unknown to others,
holed up in the midst of the capital.
The many dreams the two of us built
were all of the inner world:
what we examined were internal lives,
what we accumulated were internal treasures.
Guided by the strong arm of beauty
I worked my fingers to the bone in sculpture.

TERRIFYING EMPTINESS

Mother had been dead for a long time.
Before or after Admiral Tōgō's death
father died, whom I hadn't expected to.
Chieko's madness thrived,
sick for seven years, she died.
I used up all my energy,
in the flow of vacant months and days
I searched for Chieko who was dead.
That Chieko was my support,
that Chieko was my gyro,
became clear when she died.
Chieko's body disappeared;
Chieko became a universal being
and was always there, yes,
but I no longer could grasp her with my hands or hear her
    voice.
Flesh is truth.
Alone in my studio
I felt I was going to rip at any moment
like unmounted Chinese paper.
I always had a hollow in some part of my body
and my soul's balance was strained.
I still could toss down kegs of saké
but there was no saké that filled the emptiness.
Oddly, I walked about the streets, reeling,
when asked, edited books,
wrote poems in a strange direction,
discovered the pork cutlets of America-ya,
nibbled pickled scallions ten cents a bottle,
and passed the time with a cremator.

ANTINOMY

COOPERATIVE COUNCIL

A cooperative council was going to be set up
to convey people's wishes upward, I was told.
A man whom I had long respected came one night,
talked at length about the faults of the nation as it was,
and told me to become a member.
It wasn't an age when one could be surprised at abruptness.
If people's wishes could be conveyed upward,
I had a mountain of things I wanted conveyed upward.
In the end I became a member.
Once it begins to turn,
all the cogs move, like it or not.
Would people's wishes brought in by individuals
be conveyed upward?
A weird sort of pressure, on the contrary,
pressed down from above.
The cooperative council became an organization
that followed a certain will.
From the fifth floor where the council was,
I could see the mausoleum-like Diet.
The poem in which I mentioned the mausoleum-like Diet
was returned from a newspaper with a red mark.
The council had a suffocating air,
the wild animal inside me
was poisoned by the smell of bureaucracy
and roared, every night, toward a deserted land.

THE DAY OF PEARL HARBOR

What I heard before the declaration of war
was that there was a battle near Hawaii.
At last we're going to fight in the Pacific.
Listening to the Imperial Proclamation I trembled.
At this grave moment
my brains were distilled by an alembic,
yesterday became a remote past,
the remote past became now.
The Emperor in danger:
that phrase alone
determined everything for me.
The childhood grandfather was there,
father and mother were there.
The family clouds and mists of my boyhood days
rose and filled my room.
My ears were crammed with ancestors' voices:
His Majesty! His Majesty!
my consciousness panted, reeled.
Now I can only give myself up.
I'll protect His Majesty.
I'll give up the poetic and write poems.
I'll write a record.
I'll prevent the wastage of compatriots, if possible.
That night, in Komagome Heights where Jupiter shone large,
simply, seriously, so did I decide.

ROMAIN ROLLAND

As I took a deep, quiet breath
alone in a corner of my studio,
the heart of the broad, large world
wet me like tears.
A gentle, strong, warm hand
was put softly on my shoulder.
I raised my eyes, and Romain Rolland
was still in his frame.
The Association of Friends of Romain Rolland:
it was a gathering of friends
who wished to learn human love and respect,
spiritual freedom and exaltation.
Romain Rolland seemed to say:
"Don't you still think seriously
about the essence of *patriotisme?*
Can't you still see *la vérité?*
Can't you live above *pêle-mêle?*
I love your old roguish self better
than you now, so earnest."
The siren that sounded then
instantly turned me in the direction of the Palace.
Its power was as strong as instinct.
Two colors of poems were born to me.
One was printed,
the other wasn't.
I wrote both rebelliously.
Pitying my imbecile soul myself,
all the same, I went on recording.

IMBECILITY

Whenever I got some money, as if by routine
late at night I'd leave home.
Instead of applying a scalpel
to the throbbing pus piled up in my heart
I'd head for a bar in a shabby section of town.
"Pa, is Japan going to win like this?"
"She will."
"I get drafted during the day, you know. They force us to do
    impossible things."
"That's right. It's all impossible."
"Hey, old pal in the corner. Let's have a drink."
"It's not easy for a turner, either. I've got to go to Osaka to
    buy a tool."
"Don't talk loud. *They*'re fussy, you know."
"Pa, tell me the truth, are we going to win like this?"
"We will."
At two o'clock in the morning I'd go home.
Hurling myself at each electric pole.

END OF THE WAR

With my studio completely, cleanly burnt up,
I came to Hanamaki, Ōshū.
There, I heard that broadcast.
Sitting upright, I was trembling.
Japan was finally stripped bare,
the people's heart fell, down to the bottom.
Saved from starvation by the occupation forces,
they were barely exempt from extinction.
Then, the Emperor stepped forward
and explained that he was not a living god.
As days passed,
the beam was taken out of my eyes,
and before I knew it, the sixty years' burden was gone.
Grandfather, father, and mother
returned again to their seats in distant Nirvana,
and I heaved a deep sigh.
After a mysterious deliverance
there's only love as a human being.
The celadon of a clear sky after rain
is fragrant in my capacious heart
and now, serene, with nothing left,
I enjoy fully the beauty of the desolate.

BY THE HEARTH

REPORT (to Chieko)

Japan has completely changed.
That coarse overbearing class
whom you detested, trembling,
has, at any rate, ceased to exist.
I said "Completely changed,"
but it's a change from without
(they call it the re-education of Japan),
not an explosion from inside,
the lively new world that you hoped for
at the risk of your life—
that it wasn't obtained from within,
I am ashamed before you.
You sought true freedom.
What you sought so hard
living in the iron enclosure where you could seek nothing,
drove you in the end out of the consciousness of this world
and destroyed your mind.
I think of your sufferings now.
Japan has changed in form,
but it's painful to report to you
a change that's devoid of your sufferings.

MOUNTAIN WOODS

Now I am in mountain woods.
My innate tendency to segregate myself doesn't seem curable,
but my life has been liberated nevertheless.
I'm determined to take root in a village society
and soon to connect the world to the village.
The intense charm of soil has captivated me,
and I have known the heart of the people beating time on the
    ground.
Beauty, abundant in nature,
nourishes and saves people.
I had never imagined
that such heart-calming days were possible.
Because I have seen a sickening amount of my own imbe-
    cility,
I accept pleasantly any appraisal of my achievement,
I listen innocently to a thousand accusations that whip me.
If it's a social convention,
I'll be glad to submit to the extreme penalty.
Poems are born naturally,
my passion for sculpture burns ever more fiercely,
and I communicate every day with masters of ancient times.
I never try to engage in strenuous struggles,
but I never rest, I inch ahead,
and when I stop walking, that day is the end.
The framework of Japan, not any other country,
exists sternly in mountain woods.
Our country's reason for being in the world
must be based on this framework.
Maple branches are burning in the hearth.
Today I talked with a charcoal burner about dairy farming.
May rain falls ceaselessly,

in the quiet village which has finished riceplanting
cuckoos are making chordal ·dots.
The past is remote, and so is the future.

Prose

A BUNDLE OF LETTERS
LEFT UNMAILED

from Paris

"Take care of yourself, keep discipline, and work hard,"
father repeated the same old words in his letter the other
day. When I returned to my studio after eating supper out
and read this letter, I could vividly see the white-bearded
face of my father in a small thatched house in Komagome
surrounded by layers of luxuriating deep green foliage,
stringing together these words, each arising from the bottom
of his heart, in the middle of smoke from mosquito-killing
incense, under an old lamp that has burnt light brown. That
night I had planned to visit Miss X in Montmartre and go
with her to a mysterious cafe called Néant; but suddenly I
felt chills, sent her a telegram to cancel the meeting, and,
staying put, alone, on a chair, thought about various things
all night. Father and son indeed have to carry on a war from
which no truce is possible. If the father is strong, he
degrades his son and ends up making a so-called filial son out
of him. If the son is strong, he ends up devouring his father
like the bell-insect. No, I can't take this. There's nothing I
can do about the fact that I am a son. I don't want to
become a father, no matter what. I hear you're already the
father of two children. . . . Come to think of it now, having
sent me to foreign countries was the biggest mistake in the
old man's life. He thought I was the same as the man in the
Nara Period who sang, "Until I come with a pearl that's
sunken in the water."[1] I've become a man I myself can't
change back to what he was. I'm bound to do soon what a
bell-insect does. Rodin is the artist and human being I revere

the most. But suppose I was *his* son. When I think of this, I tremble with fear of the sin of having eaten the apple!

Now the painter Van Dongen's exhibition is on at Bernheim Jeune's shop that you know. There are sixty-four oil paintings, eleven water colors, one *pastel*, three sculptures, and nine porcelains. Except that Kees Van Dongen is a painter originally from Holland, who frequently shows his works at independent exhibitions in spring and exhibitions in the fall, I know nothing about what he's like and so on. I recall, though, seeing several of his oil paintings earlier at the same shop and secretly turning away as if I had glimpsed a different world. Now, he has exposed his entire self with swirls of flaming colors. I wish I could show it to you, show it to you.

He's a color-maniac. He's a man who slaps, slaps on the canvas the violent movements of intense feelings that lie stagnant in our hearts, but which we can't articulate or write out. The power with which he puts colors on the canvas with all his bodily strength is that of a *pitcher* throwing a steel ball. The primary colors almost piercing the canvas conflict with one another and, trembling delicately, emit noises inaudible to the ear. He uses utterly raw colors to the full. Scarlet, indigo, black, silver ash, violet, purple. These stick to large canvases in large doses. He isn't softhearted like a *pointilliste*, in whose work colors are supposed to keep some distance from one another but blend, thereby creating an illusion of some kind. Blood-red lips, indigo hair, deep-green eyes—these acquire a disharmonious balance and maintain their own positions while fighting with each other. The harmony between these colors suggests not lovers holding each other's arms, but enemies facing each other from trenches. It's a harmony that remains uncollapsed through a balance of power. It's the harmony of *gothique* architecture where powers press against each other, or the harmony of Wagner through the full use of *false relations*. I wonder how those pigeonlike artists in Japan would react to see these paintings. These are, you see, a little stronger than beans used as pellets.

Van Dongen often paints vaudevillians. There's a painting of a female lion-tamer. The golden lion with his large mouth open is rubbing his huge body against the woman. The woman, glass beads sewn into the skirts of her purple-blue gown, bare breasts shining silver like the snow on the *Pyrénées* mountains, whip gripped firmly in pale-green glove, stands, facing front, against a background of chiaroscuro in *outremer*. Her dignified beauty, her large eyes accentuated with blue eye-shadow. Placed next to this, most ancient queens in paintings will shrink into ordinary mortals.

In sharp contrast, perhaps, there is a straightforward, pure-water-like portrait of an old man. In primary colors toned down one notch, a child-faced old fogey, his hands placed on his lap, is delineated without reservation. There's a child. There's the sea. There's the sky. There are cultivated fields. There are flowers. There are the streets of Paris. But in these pictures there's no voice of joy and pleasure. There are forms of joy and pleasure. Through the forms of joy and pleasure, extreme melancholy is silently staring at us. It's here that we get scared. The false pretense of *énergie* covering fatigue, boredom, and cruelty underneath is spelled out. Degas made us feel the misery of life by painting dancers, but he didn't go beyond the realms of piteous feelings or nonresistance, or else innocence, so his paintings didn't make us taste unnatural, intense contradictions as these do. When I saw, in the painting of a triumphant singer wearing a flamelike *cadmium* costume on her amply mature flesh, a small rose of *garance* stuck into her breast, I was touched. I must have been touched, yes, because I stepped away from the appreciation of the painting. But it did touch me, and there's nothing I can do about it. Van Dongen is a painter of the age to come. He's at least a friend of ours.

I went to see the exhibition this afternoon as well, and my head is still excited. A lingering sense of painful pleasure, like that after a moxa treatment, is very reluctant to leave me.

What are you painting now? Please do not forget the *simplicité* of mind you had when you were clumsy in technique. That's why we remember Egypt and do not forget Assyria.

from Paris

I must tell you that it was a terrible mistake of mine to rent a studio in a place called Rue Campagne Première. This is the very spot where many Japanese painters lived in the past, and even now several friends of mine are here. That explains why new arrivals from Japan end up coming here without meaning to. But it's where only uninteresting, uninteresting foreigners live.[2] The next time you run into someone planning to come to Paris, advise him not to come to a place like this. When night comes I become terribly lonesome no matter what I do, and can't stay in my studio. Hearing Montmartre! Montmartre! I always run out. If you rent a studio, it has to be in Montmartre. Vaudevilles, theaters, night stalls, cafes, wine, women, *apaches.* It's a night's labyrinth filled with colors, filled with music. Just walking the streets of Montmartre, I get intoxicated. Because naked human emotions you can't see elsewhere are found everywhere here. When I think of my studio under its bright electric lights, I feel awful. No, I can't stand it. I can't stand writing a letter like this. Bye.

from Paris

Last night, at the usual cafe on the corner, as usual, we painters living in the same section of town naturally got together and stayed up late. I ended up getting furious about Dongen's painting. I was surprised that, except for one or two, most Japanese painters studying here are, contrary to what you might expect, *académique*. After a good deal of debate, we got past Dongen by agreeing on something like what he intended is interesting. If this was the time when Manet and Monet came to the fore, these guys would say, "What Manet and Monet *intended* is interesting"—at this thought I couldn't help smiling. I'd like to write about the content of the debate, but it would strike you as too absurd, so I won't.

The streets of Paris are now at the peak of beauty. The *marronniers* lining the streets, having turned red, have exactly the same color as the ancient forests that Menard paints. Above them, with a thin veil in between, the clear blue sky shimmers. In the midst of that blueness you can see the white dome of the observatory. The black bell towers of Notre Dame, like the two horns of a giant snail, look down at the world below. The half hazy Eiffel Tower stands on tiptoe, stretching itself, above an unexpected roof. Across the city the Seine flows, wavering. The plane trees on the riverbanks constantly shed their silver leaves onto the laundry boats. Far beyond the golden pegassuses on the Aléxandre Bridge, above the hill of Montmartre, you can see the cathedral of Sacré Cœur gleam white. The so-called society of Paris has just entered its *saison*. In the evening twilight that extends over three hours, receiving equal amounts of the light of the sky and the light of the gaslights, beautiful people in evening dress call out for cabs at cross-streets. When I take a walk around this time, I feel anew that I *am* in Paris. Then, the fragrance of the special, indescribable air of this city presses upon me from everywhere. The familiar sensation of deeply inhaling this elusive fragrance! But then, suddenly realizing how *fugitive* this feeling is going to be, I feel sad. By some means, I'd like to feel always and truly that I am now in Paris. I'd like to be sure that my body has entered part of the map of Paris. If I can't do this, my life in Paris will all be a dream. All empty. Ah, I am dreaming.

from Paris

I'm alone. I'm alone.

What am I in Paris for? The terrifying *crimson* smile of Paris gives me endless solitude. The voices of pleasure and joy in the streets of Paris are about to throw me into the bottomless well of melancholy. You've been to a zoo, haven't you? And didn't you feel solitude when you looked at the face of the tiger, the lion, the deer, or the crane? Weren't you scared by the cold *indifférence* that denies any communication between their hearts and yours? Whenever I saw a tiger's eyes I was saddened by the fate we shared, that we would never be able to speak to each other. I couldn't bear that unnatural, miserable comicality. I was astounded by the coldness of humans who hadn't suspected from time immemorial that something was wrong, even when such a strange thing existed in broad daylight. That's it. That's why I'm suffering from a bone-piercing sadness in the middle of voices of pleasure and joy in Paris every day. The white people have always said that the Orientals are a race possessed of a core. To me, the white race is a riddle that will never be solved. I can't even comprehend the slight movements of their fingers. Even while I'm hugging and caressing them, I only feel I'm holding a stone or a corpse. I'm often tempted to stab a *couteau* into their pure-white, waxlike chests. There's a metal net placed around me. No matter what kind of jolly conversation or relaxed group I get into, this metal net gets in my way. An ocean fish shouldn't enter a river, a river fish shouldn't enter an ocean. No good. I'd like to come home as soon as possible and rub my heart rustling, rustling, against someone else's.

I'm lonesome, I tell you.

from Paris

Don't you tell me that art is the *Œdipe-Roi* who can solve that riddle. Perhaps it is. But I'm afraid of learning its solution. I don't want to unwittingly make mother my empress and make her wander, blinded, in the fields. But when I see Rodin's sculpture a flower blooms in my heart. If no one were around, I'd sleep holding his marble *Nymphe.* I feel like Rodin's women are actually made from my rib. I can't for the life of me believe that he *made* them. Rodin is someone who's holding a plough and digging the earth. He's someone who knows what's buried where. He's someone who digs it up and brings it to the people. He's a broker who exists between nature and man. Well, it doesn't matter. *Santa Notte!*

from Paris

The other day I saw an exhibition of Rodin's drawings. I was moved in a manner I won't be able to describe completely in simple words. We are at times in danger of falling into *banalité,* and, without constantly smelling an intense fragrance like this, would lose the strength for improvement. I guess there were about a hundred fifty or sixty drawings. Most of them are those done in a large sketchbook with a pencil—some drawn with a pencil, rubbed with fingers, and lightly colored. Every one of them is a woman's body. Besides, each one is extreme. In Japan any one of these would come under the care of the Metropolitan Police Board.[3] Imagine. In a steamy, hot, closed room green slender smoke rises straight from the tip of a *Manila* cigar. You blow a whiff of breath at the root of that thread of smoke. It will coil itself, get entangled, stretch itself, and again begin to rise noiselessly—it's that beauty. The lines that make up the women Rodin draws are just like that. These women are made up of dreamy swirls of mysterious, live, slender lines like that smoke. Looking at these drawings I feel that special kind of fragrance and heat that comes out of the human skin. It's as if my own body became twisted with the *mouvements* of these women. I dare say that no art since ancient times has ever managed to express, through the *morbidezza* of the flesh, the limitless magic of the female body as powerfully as these. It's the secret of nature that can come out not in sculpture, no, not in oil painting, not of course in watercolor, either, but only in pencil and through light coloring. When I look at these, I feel Rodin again has dug up something. Why is it that I lack animal electricity so? I may be repeating myself, but I'd like to stab a knife into a taut female breast and drink the blood that spurts out. Again, the winter comes. Whew, slap, slap, goes the window curtain.

BACK FROM FRANCE

In the French painting world now there's no single great master who can dominate a whole generation. People like Collins and Laurens who are relatively well known in Japan, too, are, to be sure, the so-called top-ranking masters over there as well, but there are many others like them in France. But the picture Collins painted of a nude woman lying in a field, which is in the Luxembourg Palace (everyone knows about it because there are copies in Japan), is an absolute masterpiece. It is certainly far superior to similar paintings by Bouguereau.

Over there now a painter by the name of Van Dongen is painting with intense colors. His assertion is that the only thing a painting should do is to affect the viewer in one powerful way, and looking at his picture of flowers, you feel as if you were face-to-face with a picture by Kōrin.

Hearing this, some people over here will conclude at once, "That's the influence of Japanese art." I don't think it is so. The same is true of the relationship between Whistler and traditional Japanese painting. The painting styles of these people didn't come to acquire the forms they have because of Japanese art. Whether Japanese art existed or not, the heads of these people had already contained the buds of what later emerged in their works. The only thing Japanese art did was to stimulate them somewhat.

When you look at Dongen's paintings, the impressionist method advocated by Manet and Monet looks quite mild, and you're puzzled how such a method could have stirred such a controversy. In France now there are painting methods that have gone to such extremes.

In sculpture Rodin is the one to be mentioned above all. But Maillol has made some good things. He doesn't do too many big things, but his small shapes contain evidently full, explosive power. Many of them are statues of women.

I like Egyptian sculpture. The technique is extremely *primitive*, rough-hewn, and it doesn't pay attention to squirrelly details, but in the way it looks thrown out unfinished, it has the sort of life that presses upon you. The material is mainly red granite, and deities and kings are carved out of it.

Marble gives an excessively soft, smooth feeling, so, depending on the subject, it may at times hurt the intention of your work. Even someone like Rodin appears to have given adequate attention to the relationship between what he wanted to express and the material he used.

The mention of marble reminds me. Referring to Mr. Kitamura Shikai's *Tekona* shown at the exhibition of the Ministry of Education the other day, one critic said that the ability to carve something like that out of such a stone deserved praise. When I read it I was alarmed that those who pass as critics nowadays have so little professional knowledge. The Japanese today who have to rely on criticisms of such critics are in big trouble.

A LAST GLANCE AT THE THIRD MINISTRY OF EDUCATION ART EXHIBITION

1

November 24. Well now, this is the day I'm supposed to run some errand. This is the day I've had something stored away at the bottom of my heart. That was the feeling I'd had since morning, but I couldn't remember what it was, and, leaving that sickly feeling quietly alone, I went out to see a friend of mine at Sakuragi-chō whom I had promised to visit. At his house, the talk at one point turned to the Ministry of Education Art Exhibition. Oh yes, that's it, that's it. That was the errand. I saw it at long last, and threw away the sickly feeling that had been dogging me for some time. At the same time I felt as if it was a more serious affair, so it was like when you start to say something, the other party responds, and you find nothing to say.

"This is the last day of *the* exhibition, isn't it?"

"So it's ending. You've been badmouthing it so much, you must feel better now. How about going to see it again to give a grand finale to your badmouthing? It will be another year before you can do it again."

"I understand why you say badmouthing, but I don't mean to. Anyway, now that you told me this is the last day, I'm already beginning to miss it. Why don't you come along with me? You better look at your own painting in the light of that place once again."

"Leave me out of it. I'm sick and tired of listening to you say, right in front of my own painting: 'Quit painting for a while. Then, perhaps, you might improve.' Let me have my say, too: Stop writing those worthless mumblings strung out in thirty-one syllables.[1] 'Cause you're better at it than we are at painting."

"I completely agree. Whatever you do, your hand does things traitorous to your head."

The rain that was falling desultorily began to turn into a serious affair. To eyes and ears that had become used to the clear autumn sky that had lasted for quite some time, the misty woods and the sounds of wooden clogs were as delightful as something rare. My friend's ticket in my pocket, I went alone to the exhibition hall at Takenodai.

When I reached the avenue between the music school and the art school, I stopped, without meaning to, to stare. The new building of that wrongheaded, shabby, *gothique* wooden art school was gleaming in half-transparent aquamarine amber in front of the velvety woods of Ueno. The sound of the rain hitting my umbrella was pleasantly rhythmical in its inimitable *basse* tone. Somehow my various organs today were fresh as if newly bought. Narrowing my eyes and trying to protect this freshness as best I could, I went up to the front of the No. 2 building.

"Give us your umbrella over here," a greasy voice whammed me on the back. The place was, as before, like a train station. At the dumb, square entrance hung a lackluster, lobster-brown curtain parted and tied up at certain spots, like the one you see at the entrance-exit of the freight department of Mitsukoshi. Up front was also a lobster-brown curtain, wrinkled. In front of it was placed a bonsai of a tall, scrawny pine tree. You went through a gate like the one you have to go through to be out on the *platform* and, looking at the pale, absentminded face of a cop, turned left. A sheet of paper I hadn't seen before was posted on the curtain to the right. Written on it splendidly were the names of the winners of second, third, and other prizes. In front of it stood a couple of gray people. There was no one at the catalogue sales desk underneath.

It was hushed. Several men in overcoats were shuffling along, slithering their feet as if they were out to steal something. The rain was drumming on the roof as monotonously as some mindless festival music. Its tone resembled that of the "badger music" you heard at winter midnight in the countryside. A lukewarm chill seeped into my body through the pores, making me shudder. My feet walked about unconsciously, randomly. My eyes could see, but it was as if I had come to another world: I couldn't understand things.

A dog like a Chinese lion is barking at someone, while somewhere behind the rock a woman as pretty as a candy figure is looking in a mirror. You turn back, and there's a mound; lying about next to it are a large number of monkey-like things that are larger than the mound. You pass through the room where the blue light from the ceiling has painted the face of a woman guard green, and in a lowered area is placed a large mound of porcelain. Near our feet clouds are flying. I look at a spot where a couple of people are standing about: a woman in the Genroku style like the one I saw at a picture-book store when I was still attending elementary school is doing something. She has pink dots here and there.

I looked out of the dark room into the next room: one of the woman guards was combing her colleague's hair. A seated woman was humming *Echigo Jishi*, accompanied by the samisen sound she made with her voice. Everyone looked puzzled as though duped by a fox. Passing a long corridor, startled by a big eye looking at an arrow, I came to a large room. Soiled nobles were doing some brisk Nō chanting; pasted beyond them was a pressed picture of a sister cut out pale blue. Wondering if it wasn't a decorated battledore racket, I rolled my eyes along and came upon a spot where I could see a mountain like Mount Akagi. I looked close, and the mountain turned out to be a mirage, with the real mountain and river seen below it. I wished the mirage would dissipate anon so I might see what was beyond the landscape below, but it didn't seem willing to. I stopped waiting and turned to look to the left—well, it had to be India: there were three pure-white, beautiful women. Completely charmed by them, I became absent-minded a while. No matter how charmed I might become, there was nothing I could do about it if it was India. With some decision I stepped into the next room and almost brushed against cedar leaves—which turned out to be a picture. A cedar tree jumped out of it, quite out of tune with the rest, like a drum struck amid two-string lutes, sickeningly. My feet, to whose discretion I'd left my body, came to an unusually bright room. As if out in the sea on a windy day, I could see white waves in all directions. Or else, as if you'd gone out in the urban part of New York on a Monday, it was like washed white sheets hung in many directions. My brain felt odder and odder, so I decided to take a rest in the lounge.

2

I was served scalding hot black tea in the lounge, and my brain cleared up. I looked out of the lounge, and just then, the *Laborer* (by Ogiwara Morie) turned to look toward me, chin in hand. Startled, I stopped my hand that was putting a cookie in my mouth. Looking closer, I saw that he wasn't looking at me; with nothing particular to look at, he was simply staring, eyes wide open. It was when the summer sun beat down on you and everything cast a clear shadow on the earth. A laborer who had been battling the earth with a pick, not knowing it was a war he could never win, was giving his tired body some rest to regain his strength, perhaps. Or, knowing full well that it wouldn't work, but with the abandon of a man who couldn't stop once he'd embarked on something, he was determined, because he couldn't give up being a human being, to drink, eat, sleep, get violent, and yell, so that he might have a hell of a good time of it, short though his life might be; but body tired, his spirit had sagged, and sensing something serious gleaming at the unseen borders, he was searching for it in the depths of his brain. Or, lump of flesh that he was, was he perhaps letting his soul soar, his mind unthinking and pure white, in a realm of empty solitude even Zen masters can't reach? Such were the thoughts I had when my eyes were looking at the top of the marble that was a table. Now out of the lounge, I walked about to have a serious look.

The *Cat* (by Asakura Fumio) caught my eye. Its technique was reminiscent of Rembrandt Regatti's, whose work I had recently seen often in Paris. Compared with the technique used for the cat, the hands and arms behind it were extremely stiff, and troubling when looked at from the side. However, what was interesting was that Asakura had made and exhibited it to us when people these days think that an artist can't be great unless he makes ponderous, massive things. . . .

Seeing something with the author's "intentions" clearly exposed but without *la vie* is like seeing a clumsy outline; it puts you off. Art isn't interesting unless it makes you feel something without fuss, directly. If it's a sculpture, sculptural techniques, such as the *touche*, construction, the tactile sensation of the surface, and the harmony of the color sense, must at once give you a certain feeling. Something that makes you think of the technique and subject matter separately is no good. In the case of this *Cat*, its real merit doesn't lie in the comicality of a cat held up by the neck. What gives you pleasure is the way the technique recreating the flesh of a cat, the relationship between the dark and light places, the softness with which the mass of the thing is expressed, and such things give you at once the feeling of a cat even before they bring it up explicitly to your consciousness. Things like the comicality I just mentioned are matters that come up as afterthoughts. Make something mainly to produce such effects, and art begins its degradation. This *Cat*, in my eyes, fortunately doesn't seem to have been made with such thoughts. I think Asakura found a cat amusing and made a cat.

Now, this piece was amusing but had no great value because it had no depth. The cat didn't have an animal in it. It didn't have *la vie* in the true sense of the word. How did this come about? First, I'd say it was caused by the author's personality and taste. Next, his techniques were still not adequate. About the author's personality and taste, there's little I can do. As for the techniques, this cat didn't have enough *solidité*. The inadequacy made the piece shallow. Its *planes* were confused. That also reduced its depth. Its lines were not continuous. That prevented the mood from focusing. The hands behind in particular showed these defects and gave you a chilling feeling, which was worse than a *negative* sentiment.

In any event, what's interesting about this *Cat* is that Asakura has treated sculpture as sculpture. The attitude may become something to be taken for granted in a couple of years, but while many sculptures don't take it for granted, the position of the one that does rises above the rest. . . .

3

. . . a large woman covering her head and all with a sheet of cloth was peering up and beyond (*Anxiety* by Kunikata Tenkai). In the art museum at the Luxembourg Palace there is a piece in exactly the same shape, made by assembling colored stones. It's an extremely callow piece intended to show, through the fable of a woman opening a little the sheet covering her, how one secret of the world after another is discovered by mankind. I don't know what this particular woman has in mind, but it's a weird piece.

Running away from it, I saw a baby lying on the floor beyond. Behind it was a woman. Two separate pieces were installed too damned close to each other, I felt, but then I saw that these made up a single composition (*Orphan* by Mōri Moritake).[2] This, too, seemed to have a profound meaning. The baby must be the child of the woman standing behind it. The young mother who died, leaving this child, had shown up in the child's dream, perhaps, or, unable to become a buddha, had appeared as a ghost. . . .

This sculpture, too, missed the mark. The baby and the woman were merely placed there as explainers of some theatrical story. So the sculpture had no *charme* or power. . . . A sculpture that isn't interesting in a way unique to sculpture has no reason for being. . . .

There was one showing a woman lying down. When something is so patently an imitation, the repellent feeling an imitation usually arouses is dispelled (*Fatigue* by Fujii Kōyū). Rodin, in his *Danaïde,* simply scratched lines with a small chisel into the material it was made out of, marble, to represent strands of hair. The half-transparent marble and the whitish nontransparency of the chisel scratches recreate the softness of hair in the most simple, the most effective way. This woman imitated even that technique of the *Danaïde.* I don't think imitation itself is bad. Sometimes, to express a similar sentiment one may have to do something similar. Especially while a student you even copy. Or, as in the case of Maeterlinck, boldly using in one's work what is evidently someone else's techniques can at times produce some interesting effects. But unless you do this sort of thing wisely, it can ruin what may be important to you. Making this woman's hair like that of the *Danaïde* is a case in point. I'd like the author to realize that technique must change in response to the material used. This work, too, lacked *la vie*. The *plane* was not understood. I don't know if the author has the idea of *accent*, but this work shows he has none. So he made something as flabby as noodles boiled too long. Besides it lacked interesting lines. The lack of interesting lines came about because the author was lacking in his power to observe the *mouvement* of nature. . . .

4

Next to it was a dark portrait (*Portrait of Mr. Hōjō Torakichi* by Ogiwara Morie). The first time I came to this exhibition and saw this portrait, I felt for the first time that I was in touch with a work of art. . . .

I am deeply pleased that something like this has been made by the hands of a Japanese in the Japanese Nation. Needless to say, this work shows there still are many things the author must grasp in his hands, with effort. The framework has been built. Now we need walls. We need floor boards. We must make *tatami* mattresses and doors. But what's most lacking about this work is the feeling of flesh. It doesn't have *morbidezza*. . . .

Also, the color isn't good. The relationship between sculpture and the color of its material is, I think, of considerable importance. With the idea that sculpture by nature is monochromatic, the notion of color has weakened, so that there are even some sculptors who are utterly indifferent to color. But that this isn't right should be clear from the fact that the three things a human being feels—sound, color, and shape—react with one another. How can an artist, whose nerves are sensitive to the delicate points of any shape, neglect the color? . . . The author of this portrait does have some thought for color; this you can see in the not unpleasant color of the portrait. But it's also obvious that he didn't give too much attention to it. The color of this bronze is dry. It's too cold. And it seems too monotonous. One would hope to have more depth. The bronze of Rodin's busts gives you a pleasant sensation, even if you look at their color alone. The color of his material and the content of his sculpture mesh precisely. His *St. John* was in bronze, his *Kiss* in marble. The fact that plaster copies lose all the subtleties of the original sculptures has a lot to do with this. I am altogether dissatisfied that Japanese sculptors don't care much about this. . . .

5

I turned back to look, and there was this lump of metal scrap covered with ash. The impression had come from the malfunctioning of my brain: it was the one called *Pithecanthropus* (by Shinkai Taketarō),[3] which I had seen when I came here before. Trying to suppress with all my strength the same unpleasant sensation that again raised its head, I stood in front of this work in my attempt to appreciate it to the best of my ability. Several college women came in, merrily laughing—something rarely done here!—and, looking at this work from behind me, commented among themselves:

"Wait, this is the day we have the Darwin Festival, no?"

"Have you read *The Descent of Man*?"

"Wait, love. Even in Japan's art world we can now see, can't we, something like this *Pithecanthropus*—an excellent work on a solid base, *philosophical*, that has not only *heart* but also *brain*, and comes with a scientific value. When you see something like this, all the works in the past look like soap bubbles, don't they? They may look pretty, all right, but they are empty inside."

"I'd like to install this one in a zoological garden."

I could see their point. Their words seemed to have been uttered with a good understanding of the attitude of the author who made the piece. But with people behind me who *appreciated* this piece in that sense, I felt my back itch. . . .

I am someone who's never shaken by the *excentricité* of a given thing. Even when I saw for the first time the paintings of Cezanne, of course, the paintings of Van Dongen, paintings of Matisse, and sculptures of Rosso, I may have *appreciated* their virtues, but never felt in the least *choqué* by their *excentricité*. For me the meaning of the word *shocking* must have become extremely narrow. Nevertheless, the first word I wanted to utter when I saw this work was, "*Shocking.*" Why was that? I couldn't understand it myself. But when I thought about it, it occurred to me that I was *choqué* by the unconscious realization that an artist should have made this and shown it in an art exhibition—*choqué* not in the sense *esthétique*, but in the sense *morale*. But the source of the sense *morale* lay in the former, so the work was to blame. There is no other work in this exhibition hall as conceptual as this. There is also no other work that has ignored sculpture itself and turned it into a kind of puppet as this work has. There is no other work that is made with a technique based on *faux fondement* as this is. There is no other work that shows, as this does, the pretense of *flamboyant* through hands so *timide*. . . .

What jars the viewer's feelings besides is a technical bluffing of the sort one might expect from a drunken man revealing his true nature. Sargent, who is in England now, is a portrait artist known to everyone. In audacious brushwork there has been no one like him since Frans Hals. The way he quickly works out a six-foot long canvas with his brush laden with ample paint deserves true admiration. The life of Sargent's painting doesn't lie in his brushwork alone, of course, but it does get from it great enhancement of light and color. Many English painters are dazzled by that brushwork. If you go to the Academy and other exhibitions, you see countless pictures by the painters captured by it. Everyone draws back from it, has second thoughts about it, yet ends up copying its *audacity*. Nothing is as sickening as this.

When I saw this *Pithecanthropus*, I inadvertently thought of English painters holding large brushes in their trembling hands. Perhaps I have said too much of what came to my mind. I've heard that the wise are those who don't say what they think just the way they think; in this, too, I'm one of the brainless bunch.

OGIWARA MORIE,
WHO DIED

At the moment I am thinking about the art of Ogiwara Morie, who died. But no matter how I try, I can't think of him as an artist of the past, one coherent being with a definable shape. My feeling is that of someone who has awakened in the midst of a good dream and can't help thinking about what was to follow. Ogiwara was someone who was to do good work in the days to come. When I think of him, his work to be made in the future, his art yet to be seen, stimulates my brain more strongly than the works already made. In fact, my brain is full of his future works. All those future works have to be destroyed with his death—this I understand perfectly well. I understand it well, but they are nonetheless lined up firmly in my brain. His bigness, his interesting part, was all to be in the future. Yet, he died. I haven't encountered anything as unreasonable in recent years.

I became acquainted with Ogiwara only four or five years ago and began to think of him as a truly interesting man to speak to only in the summer of 1907 when he came to visit me in my lodging in Putney, in London. Even then, I talked to him only four or five times. When I went to Paris that winter, we once spent about a week together, walking, talking. Before we could meet again, he returned to Japan. I myself came back to Japan a year later. My large hands and his powerful hands met again after quite a while at the station in Shimbashi, and afterward I'd say we visited each other without much interruption.

It was in Paris that I saw his talent. It was in Tokyo that I saw him as a man. It was in my study, after his death, that I clearly saw his future works. While he was alive, I couldn't

174

perceive his existing works as separate from those in the future. The value of his future works was then contained in his existing works. Now they will be separated. To me, the whole thing has a pitiless, sad, and cruel air. But there's nothing I can do about it.

I saw him for the first time when I was in New York. I hadn't even heard of him as a painter. It all began when Yanagi Keisuke came with him to visit me in my apartment. I got the impression of an apparently egotistic, youthfully pushy man who habitually said, *"Mikeranji, Mikeranji"*[1] before we parted.

His tone was: "It's no good to see the small things by Rodin that you can get in New York. If you see those things and admire Rodin, hell, you don't understand him at all." When I heard this through my friends, I thought: "Here's a trouble-maker. Can't he savor a cup of wine when that's all he has, and savor a barrel of wine when that's all he has?" After that I didn't see much of him. When I think of it now, I simply did not know of his sufferings, that he was filled with doubts and anxieties about art. I did not know that he was about to make his move. Later I heard from Yanagi that he often said, *"What is art?"* in those days.

Not long afterward, Ogiwara went off to Paris. I heard that he had started to sculpt at the Académie Julian. I thought: "I see it now. He's a man of sculpture. He got what he wanted by turning to sculpture."

He often sent me photographs of his model sculptures. I saw them with Yanagi. We said, "There they are still, those swirls of his." After that time the traffic between us increased. About four months into my stay in London, he wrote me from Paris to say: "My head has gotten so bad I'm thinking of spending this summer in London. When I come to London, I'd like to see you."

I myself looked forward to his visit. He came. In my sec-

175

ond-floor apartment on the Thames, we spent a whole day talking. I took out a book about Egypt. He brought up the subject of a Cezanne exhibition. It was at that time that the old mistress of the boardinghouse handed down her appraisal of him: *"He has something very precious."* He stayed in London for quite a while. I went to visit him in his lodging in Tottenham. We toured museums together. We once spent half a day in a room of Egyptian sculpture. After he went back to Paris, I thought: "Well, he's a good man. An interesting artist. A true creator." He was completely different from the man I had known in New York.

That winter when I went briefly to Paris, I saw his model head in a class at the Académie Julian and knew for the first time his extraordinary talent. I thought it was a sure thing with him. Before leaving, I suggested that he make a plaster copy of it. It's the head called *Miner* among the works he's left to us.

When I moved to Paris the next year, Ogiwara was already preparing to go back to distant Japan. He wrote many letters from Japan. When he wrote, he wrote three or four letters one after another; when he didn't, he did not for as long as three months. A card of June 27 said: "Beloved Friend. Forgive my silence since last. I have an illness in my chest, extremely serious, went to spend time in Kyoto, Nara, and washed my deranged chest several times in the waves of Konan, but am not cured yet."

Later there was also this on a sheet torn from rolled paper:

"Beloved Friend M.[2] How have you been since last? At this end there's no excuse. For a time I was about to die spiritually but still keep my twilight life. The other half of hedonism is sadness. My behavior is that of a traveler wandering in a valley after sunset, fumbling his way with his feet. Blind. Not only love but life is also like a blindman. I came back, to attempt some activity. But heaven arranges things well. At once I was caught in the cold hands of fate and utterly immobilized. But my big brother kindly made a studio for me. I had to do some work. What I made with great reluctance is the *Mongaku* in a recent exhibition which won me third prize, an award to be grateful for. I'm sick in my head. It mayn't be cured forever. That's why I can't make anything exciting. When I was done I went back to my hometown. Thinking that I'd have the mountains of Shinshū cool my too feverish head. But that, too, didn't work. In half a month I came back and went to see the salaam-requiring thing called the second officially mounted exhibition. There was absolutely nothing that was interesting. Everything has vulgar smells and base airs that strike you from everywhere. Among the paintings Mr. Kuroda Seiki's was interesting, among wooden sculptures the *Kanzanshi* by Yonehara Unkai was good. Anxieties come from laziness. Determined to work hard I shut myself in the studio for two days, became ill (body), was laid up for about half a month. I went to play in Kamakura, Kotsubo, etc., and illness came back but now overall wholly recovered, the day before yesterday I started work on a bust of so-and-so but because of some urgent business he disappeared and I was left feeling as though duped by a fox. Today a suspicious woman came to model. Japanese women, especially those likely to do modeling work, are a shoddy lot. She was like looking at an Egyptian sculpture by Maillol. I made her stand and she presented such *thrilling* lines. I thought of doing the *Despair* and made her lie down on her side and she ended up looking like Rodin's *Danaide*. . . ."

So while I was in Paris the *Mongaku* was completed. A photograph came. He wrote to say he had a skin disease. When I wrote accusing words on the *Mongaku* and sent them to him, I received a letter, which said:

177

". . .Your criticism of the *Mongaku* is exactly right. I have no disagreement, no, I had probably felt the lack of inner power more than you did. But as I wrote in my previous letter various things happened in my life and even though I don't easily get beaten by most things I ran into this one thing I couldn't defeat and I've suffered a terribly embarrassing defeat. I'm continuing the battle today but continue to suffer defeat. I'm resigned that I won't be able to do anything right until I see the outcome of this war. But the longer it lasts the worse my brain gets and in time I may end up as a true man of inaction. . . . Recently, though I wouldn't say I'm crazy about it, when I get frustrated I often go to Gidayū.[3] I appreciate such unfinished products as Kumisachi, Daikichi, and Tōen, rather than the established folks like Kokiyo and Sogyō. Among the men Asadayū is interesting. I take to the warmth of his tone. Matsutarō's strings are the best under heaven. . . . Mornings I'm continuing the *Despair* for now. But I'm not doing well though doing it in the belief that I am doing well. In my mind is illness, how can my work go well? But I must do it. Yanagi has told me he's thinking of coming back in the near future. The sort of man that he is, I can't say anything about it."

I couldn't help cursing the cruel pressure of nature that was behind these sentences. Soon I too returned to Japan. The man I thought I disliked in New York had become someone I liked so much I spontaneously gripped his hands when we met in Shimbashi. After returning to Japan I saw Ogiwara's works for the first time on the stage of Mr. Seiko's "Criticism of Wooden Sculpture." He was working on that *Laborer.* There was also *Despair.* Mr. Tabari's Kōgan portrait was there, too. I couldn't suppress my joy, thinking, "The world of sculpture will become very interesting from now on." Indeed, that world was becoming a reality. We hadn't stepped into it yet, but it was right there in front of our eyes. Then it went out. The expression "There's nothing I can do about it" is indeed a cruel one.

As for my impression of Ogiwara's art since I came back to Japan, I'd like to write about it on another occasion.

A GREEN SUN

People become stuck in an unexpectedly insignificant place and suffer.

The so-called Japanese-style painters can't move forward, marked by the term "Japanese-style." The so-called Western-style painters can't, either, weighed down by oil paint on their backs. Sometimes you end up being more protective of a pawn than of the knight. Your *motiv* for that may be funny if you think about it, but when you magnify with a lens a situation where you can't move forward, and contemplate it, you may be persuaded that it *is* cruel. Meaningless confusion and the abuse of the dangerous *sonde* [probe] are the heavy tolls exacted of every artist at such a moment. In this sense, no other artists than the Japanese today place such expensive but useless stamps on their works, or have. In revolt against these heavy taxes, there may yet ensue *Anarchismus* in the art world. But the *Anarchismus* that ensues from such a situation will be reactionary. It won't be the *Anarchismus* of the *Anarchists*.

I seek absolute *Freiheit* [freedom] in the art world. Therefore, I want to recognize an infinite authority in the artist's *Persoenlichkeit* [personality]. In every sense, I'd like to think of the artist as a single human being. I'd like to regard his *Persoenlichkeit* as the starting point and *Schaetzen* [appreciate] his work. I want to study and appreciate his *Persoenlichkeit* as it is, and do not want to throw too much doubt into it. If someone sees what I think is blue as red, I'd like to start on the basis that *he* thinks it's red, and *Schaetzen* how he treats it as red. About the fact that he sees it as red, I wouldn't want to complain at all. Rather, I'd like to take as a *Angenehmer Ueberfall* [pleasant invasion] the fact that there is a view of nature different from mine, and would contemplate the extent to which he has peered into the core of nature, the extent to which his *Gefuel* [feeling] has been fulfilled. That done, I then would like to savor his *Gemuetsstimmung* [frame of mind]. This desire of my mind drives me so that it has minimized the value of *local color* which is on people's lips these days. (The expression, in English, has a couple of meanings; here, it will denote the usual one of the character of natural colors of a particular region.)[1] It is my view that for a painter to think and suffer about something like *local color* is just another way of paying for an expensive but useless stamp of the kind I mentioned before.

If my demand for absolute *Freiheit* were wrong as an attitude, all my thoughts that arise from it would be valueless. But this happens to belong in the category where there can't be any mistake. For it is not a theory, but my own feeling. Even if someone says it is wrong, I won't be able to do anything about it as long as my brain exists. So I'd like to put in words at least what I think.

I am born Japanese. Just as a fish can't live out of water, so I can't live as a non-Japanese, even if I remain quiet about it. At the same time, just as a fish isn't conscious that he's wet in the water, so at times I'm not conscious that I'm Japanese. "At times" isn't the right expression. I am more often unconscious than not. I often think I'm Japanese when I'm dealing with someone. The thought doesn't occur much when I face nature. That is, I think of it when I think of my own turf. Such a thought can't possibly occur when I have my own self thrown into an object.

My psychological state while making art is, therefore, where only one human being exists. Thoughts of things like Japan don't exist at all. I simply go ahead, thinking, seeing, and feeling as I do, regardless. The work, when you look at it later, may turn out to be so-called Japanesey. It may not. Either way, it won't bother me, the artist, at all. Even the existence of local color, in such an instance, will mean nothing.

There are quite a number of people in today's painting world who think highly of the value of local color. There seem to be even some who think that the fate of Japanese oil paints will be determined by the way the painters compromise with the local color of Japan. There also seem to be not a few people who take a step or two, then hesitate, thinking that nature in Japan has a certain inviolable set of colors peculiar to it, so that if they infringe on it, their works will immediately lose their *raison d'être*—all this prompting them to try to suppress the flaming colors and dreamlike *ton* in their hearts. Others put themselves in a harshly rigid attitude that doesn't tolerate even the view of according simple *Abschaetzung* [evaluation], while they give an absolute value to local color and treat as something out of the question all the works that have recognized different colors to any degree. And the value of local color seems to be recognized by the general public. This you can tell from the fact that the expression, "There's no such color in Japan," is accepted as a condemnatory pronouncement. I'd like to ignore this local color. Needless to say, I am saying this from the standpoint of an artist.

Even if someone paints a "green sun," I will not say it is wrong. This is because there may be a time when the sun looks that way to me, too. Simply because a painting has a "green sun" in it, I will not be able to overlook the overall value of the painting. The good or bad of the painting has nothing to do with whether the sun is green or flaming scarlet. In such a case, too, as I said before, I'd like to savor the tone of the green sun as part of the work. I will not compare the Buddhist statues of the Fujiwara Era, which are truly like "Japanese" buddhas, with those of the Tempyō Era, which have a great deal of foreign flavor added to them, and then take the former over the latter from the viewpoint of *local color*. I'd like to place one work above or below another on the basis of the amount of *Das Leben* [life]. I'd like to allow the *Persoenlichkeit* of the artist who has painted a green sun to have absolute authority.

It appears that seeing nature in Japan in light ink tones has become standard for people today. They seem to want to control everything with the tone of the overcast sky. "Fallen Leaves" by Mr. Hishida Shunsō represents one aspect of this. Even someone like Mr. Kuroda Seiki seems to be striving to Japanize (?) himself. And the public appears to regret that his Japanization has yet to reach maturity.

Among those who value local color the most is my friend, Mr. Ishii Hakutei. His taste for it comes not so much from a theoretical requirement that local color be valued as from purely Japanese taste and the classical taste rooted in his *temperament*. In this regard, his extremely sharp sensibility rejects the colors of the city today as remote from Japan's local color and chooses the water in the Marunouchi Moat, the Kasuga Field in Nara, and the banks along the Tone River. His is the happiest example of an artist's taste according with the local color of his country that is reflected in his eyes.[2] The tones he tries to paint, driven by inner demands, correspond, by themselves, to the local color of Japan that people talk about nowadays. As a result, the *Eigenheit* [peculiarity] of the immovable Japanese local color establishes itself in his sensibility. It is natural that he should become one of those who value local color the most. Accordingly, he actively inspects many works with his test tube of local color. Works with what he calls "the Western smell" are weeded out in that fashion. His *saveur* [taste] can't help influencing his painting techniques. In this, in contrast to my leaning toward *Anarchismus,* he tends toward *Monarchismus.* Even when nature is looked at in the same manner, such differences come about because of temperamental differences. Needless to say, this is not a question of which is right, which is wrong.

I do recognize deductively the existence of local color from the standpoint of appreciation. In Japanese works there is what should naturally be seen as the local color of Japan. The same is true of works by French, English, etc. But I am simply recognizing the existence of the local color, not its value. I recognize it as an accessory but not as an object for appreciation. When you make gas out of coal, you get coke. You take it because you get it. You get it even if you don't mean to. Something made by a Japanese is in the end Japanese. It ends up being Japanese. It does, even if you don't mean to make it that way. This is what's called the "rotten relationship" you can't do anything about. In appreciating a given work I'd like not to put local color into my feelings, but to savor the work as it is, allowing local color as revealed in it to have an infinite authority. Even the works in which we, today, can't see any local color will turn out to have the color of today, of the Meiji Era, when they are looked back on later—or so I'd like to think.

If you don't leave local color entirely to the *Persoenlichkeit* of the artist himself, if you instead allow the appreciator to use it as he wishes, you are in effect putting another shackle on the artist. The concept of local color is, in a strict sense, another *Allgemeine Uebereinstimmung* [universal concord]. It is something the appreciator should be free to savor, not something the artist should worry about. It is something to be commented upon after the work is finished, not something you will to create.

I'd like the artist to forget that he's Japanese. I'd like him to rid himself entirely of the idea that he is reproducing nature in Japan. And I'd like him to express on his canvas the tone of nature as he sees it, freely, indulgently, willfully. Even if his finished work produces what is the opposite of the local color of Japan that we think we see in our eyes, I will not want to reject it on that account. To the eye of someone with Chinese feelings, even nature in Japan will at times appear Chinese-style. To the eye of someone *exotisch*, even the torii of a fox shrine may appear tinged with exotic colors. A bystander has no right to complain of something with which he has nothing to do. An appreciator facing a work of art has no need to question the fact that it is different. He should simply recognize that it is different, and then try to see, on the basis of the work, whether the artist's sentiments are based on something false or on his innate sincerity. The goodness or badness of the work must come into his mind as a separate issue.

From this standpoint, I am hoping that Japanese artists will use all the *moeglich* [possible] techniques without any reservation. I pray that they will follow their inner urges of the moment and not be necessarily afraid that they may produce something non-Japanese. No matter how non-Japanese, a work made by a Japanese can't avoid being Japanese. Gauguin went as far as Tahiti and created non-French colors, but his works are, when you think of it, not in the Tahitian style but in the Parisian style. Whistler lived in France and for a while indulged in *nostalgie* for Japan, but he is indisputably *Angel-Saechsisch* [Anglo-Saxon]. Turner painted the streets of London in Italian colors, but when you think of it now, the colors with which he painted Italian nature were in the end English in style.

Monet did not try to reproduce the local color of France; he tried to recreate nature. Of course, the public did not accept his as French colors. Worse, they did not accept them as natural colors, either. He was denounced because he had painted tree leaves sky-blue. Nevertheless, when you look at his works now, they have an unmistakably French touch of the sort no one from any other country could have. All this is like a fish having a watery touch. Something like that is not gained by effort, but comes with the thing itself. When you try to obtain something like that through effort, the degradation of art begins.

While I think the shrine fence painted scarlet beautiful, sometimes I am also entranced by the electric advertisements of Jintan. That's when creative fervor is boiling in my head. When there is no creative fervor, I am irritated to no end by the random confusion of the city today. There always live in my mind bugs of these two different stripes. Similarly, while I admire so-called Japanese taste, I am also captivated by non-Japanese tastes. Also, while I regard Japan's local color to some extent as other people do, in my heart of hearts I reduce its value to zero. So when I look at things Westernized, I do not in the least feel repelled by their Westernization. Even if I see a green sun, I do not feel offended.

I have ended up writing down my thoughts in their confused state. All I wanted to do was to say a word on local color, which I think is of little import but of which the world at large makes a big deal. I passionately hope that Japanese artists will see not Japan but nature, will not give a damn about local color that has been turned into a set rule, but will express recalculated color tones as they please.

No matter what willful things we may do, all we'll have left after our death will be works only Japanese can make.

THOUGHTS

If someone says to me, Your art is an imitation, I can insist from the bottom of my heart that it isn't.

If someone says to me, Your art is false, I can insist from the bottom of my heart that it isn't.

If someone says to me, Your art is rootless, I can insist from the bottom of my heart that it isn't.

If someone says to me, Your art is a concept, I can insist from the bottom of my heart that it isn't.

If someone says to me, Your art is an outer crust, I can insist from the bottom of my heart that it isn't.

But if someone says to me, Your art has no power, I can only keep quiet.

For the presence or absence of power in this context is the reflection of the viewer's power.

The relationship between my art and myself is much closer than what a debate on the presence or absence of power may suggest. It is absolute.

When someone says to me, Your art has no power, I become mortally afraid, while at the same time feeling grateful for that honest word. . . .

THE SCULPTOR
MR. GUTZON BORGLUM

I will tell you a story that's already ten years old.

For the first time since I was born, I left the land of Japan, and after a forlorn trip of about a month, early one morning I was ejected, alone, onto the sooty platform of Grand Central Station in New York. I suddenly thought of my distant father and mother and couldn't hold back my tears. I was such a spoiled kid of twenty-four who, brought up in school, didn't know anything about the affairs of the world. I certainly didn't see how from then on I could seek food, how I could study, in the fierce life of this bustling city of America. About to step into the terrible battles that rose and crashed in front of me, I cannot tell you how painfully I missed my still sleepy hometown, the natural phenomena and human affairs there, which, at that moment, seemed to me as peaceful as a garden with grass growing in it.

While still struggling with my own uneasy, timid mind, I was lucky enough to find work as an assistant to an unusually fine sculptor in America, Mr. Gutzon Borglum. Mr. Borglum is still utterly unknown in Japan. It also appears that the first thing people think of when they hear America mentioned is that it has only unworthy artists. Also, it happens that my memories of Mr. Borglum are the fondest I have. So I'd like to talk about this sculptor.

When I left Japan, Professor Iwamura Tōru gave me letters of introduction written to the sculptors French and McNeill. These letters were the only things I had to rely on. But even though the two gentlemen courteously received me, neither offered to employ me as an assistant. Mr. French was the doyen of the American sculpture world at the time

188

and was ranked with Saint-Gaudens, who died shortly afterward. Mr. McNeill was a rising star already attracting a lot of attention. The approximately $250 I had brought from home decreased day by day. There was no way to make money. Once I received from Mr. French an invitation to the great dinner party of the American Sculptors' Association, but I had to decline to attend it. The embarrassment I felt because of this is something that still empties my head of blood when I remember it.

One day an earlier graduate of my alma mater, Shirataki Ikunosuke, told me that there was an American sculptor by the name of Borglum who had shown an exceptionally fine work at an exposition. In those days, even in my difficult circumstances, I used to go almost every day to the Metropolitan Museum of Art, where I was overjoyed to see the *St. John*, a head by Rodin. So I looked for Mr. Borglum's work in the room of American sculpture. Somehow I did not like the sculpture of that country, even feeling sick when looking at the new-style works by someone like MacMonnies. But then a bluish, finely hued, large, cast-metal sculpture of a group of madly galloping horses caught my eye. A powerfully built naked man had jumped out to grab the neck of a ferocious horse. The overall composition was triangular, and its extremely violent movement shook me up. Wondering what it was, I looked at the plaque; it said, "Diomedes' Mare." It was a work by Gutzon Borglum.

When I saw it, I suddenly decided that the sculptor of this man-eating horse was certain to make me his assistant. The desire to meet him flared up. In the midst of many other sculptures that were fine but cold, this one had passion sealed into it. It felt entirely different. That night, lying on my lonesome bed, I went ahead and wrote a letter to him. In shaky sentences, I wrote only what I felt, said that I wanted very much to work for him as an assistant, and asked him to hire me. I was timid in those days, but some mysterious power pushed me. The next morning I tried to mail the letter, but something got stuck in my chest, and I couldn't put it in the mailbox. So I thought again, obtained a letter of introduction from Mr. French, and enclosed it in the same envelope, which finally gave me the courage to mail the letter. It was at the end of April in New York. The trees in the streets were already budding, at times there was thunder and rain, and mists rose. I was restless and worried while waiting for a reply. Yanagi Keisuke often came to visit and console me. A week later things worked out in such a way that I was finally able to visit Mr. Borglum.

On Thursday morning in early May, I went to Grand Central Station by subway and walked a few blocks to the gate of Mr. Borglum's studio, which was on East 38th Street. My heart began to shake; trying to calm down, I entered the gate and walked about twenty yards on an asphalt path with geraniums planted on both sides. At its end was a large glass double door that was closed. Trees like "palm bamboos" planted there were growing well, adding a tasteful touch. I pushed the bell. A man in his late twenties, with a rounded back and in gray work-clothes, opened the door and took my calling card inside. I was called in at once. I entered, and it was a very large studio with a high ceiling, bright, a neat wooden floor—these were the things I perceived, but I was too excited to notice what was placed there. I was led to a corner of the room where there was an enclosure about nine by twelve—what might be called a *cozy corner* under a staircase.

A man suddenly thrust his hand out, gripped my hesitant hand so strongly that it almost hurt, made sure what my name was, announced his own, and rapidly said things like: "I am delighted by the sense of justice and taste of the Japanese people. When did you begin to study sculpture? When did you come to New York? Do you understand English well?" It was Mr. Borglum. He looked at the photographs of my own sculptures that I showed him, singled out the one of the *Kikugorō V*, and said, "This is a little better." He was a bit shorter than I, but had a rock-sturdy body and thick fingers. His powerful build from neck to face and the beauty of the bluish-black eyes that stared at you while he talked were particularly notable. I had assumed that anybody bald was old and at first thought he was quite advanced in age, but in several minutes I made certain that he wasn't even forty yet. He spoke, chopping his sentences into short phrases, straightforwardly, bluntly. "I'll give you an answer next Wednesday evening. Today you might as well see our works." With this, he put on an overcoat his assistant brought him and went out. I impatiently waited for the next Wednesday and went to his place that evening.

"Do you know how hard an assistant's work is? Can you put up with it? But if you are truly determined to become an artist, you can give it a try. Your work, schoolwork, no good," Mr. Borglum said, mixing in pidgin English so that I might understand.

"I think I understood what you said, sir. I have a strong body, and I can do anything. Please allow me to live here," I asked him again. He said he couldn't let me live with him, but I could come to his place at nine o'clock in the morning every day and work until evening; he would allow me to use his models on Monday, Wednesday, and Thursday nights so that I could do charcoal drawing with everybody else. He then suddenly slapped me on the back and shouted, "*Cheer up!*" I felt the amorphous and irritating thing that had become a habitual occupant of my head suddenly drop away. In a fierce fighting mood, I went back to my apartment.

For the next four months, I worked every day at my

191

teacher's place for a wage of six dollars a week. My body becomes feeble in the summer, however; I gave in to the terrible heat of New York finally, in August, and had to stop going. In those days everything I saw and heard was a great surprise to me. My teacher's life was no exception at first. In most cases the program for the activities of the next day was set the previous evening, and according to that schedule he worked, made visits, received guests, and had a rest. I had been used to the way Japanese artists lived, so I was surprised that he still could do artwork under such circumstances. He mostly dictated his letters to his assistant, who typed them on the spot, added his signature, and mailed them. It was a dizzyingly busy life. But I soon learned that in the midst of his ferocious activities my teacher had an ample inner life.[1]

He had spent his youthful years with cowboys and hordes of horses in the wild plains of the American West, then went to England and France to study sculpture. He is one of the sculptors most deeply affected by Rodin. But Mr. Borglum is American to the core. He is a man remarkably well equipped with that special greatness all good Americans have. He has thoughts and personal traits that are common to Lincoln, Whitman, and Emerson. He can live with straightforward honesty in the fierce swirls of a tough life, dealing in an extremely natural fashion with artificial civilization. He recognizes greatness in daily life and accomplishes great things with Lincolnesque humor.

Among his sculptures, other than the *Mare* that I mentioned before, the *Ruskin* is the most famous. It is a full-figure statue made from memory of a man whom he met when the latter was old. It is only a foot and a couple of inches tall, but it is an unusually fine piece in the American sculpture world. It has much more inner spirit than the clever, finely executed pieces of Trubetskoy, who is known worldwide for his small portrait statues. It shows Ruskin wrapped in a blanket in a chair with a book in his hand. My teacher was particularly fond of this statue, and I often saw him caressing it when he was alone. He also had a seven-foot-tall group statue entitled *I Play the Flute But No One Dances*, but the *Nero*, which was less than a foot tall, I think, most fully expressed man's animality. The piece that especially moved me was a female nude statue called *Budding*, which he started to make while I was with him.

Often, when he returned from outside, my teacher would suddenly take off his hat, gloves, and jacket, and, stripped down to his shirt, jump on someone and begin to wrestle. He was as good at fencing as at wrestling. After exerting himself to the full, he would wash his face and begin his work at once. Once, for a bronze statue, I became the model. One day the client for the statue, who was a woman, came and saw me standing. When I heard her say, "He's a good young man," I felt deeply embarrassed and almost trembled. Noticing this, my teacher looked me straight in the eye and said he himself had done modeling in the past. What an encouragement that was!

On another occasion, I voiced my dissatisfaction with someone's sculpture. My teacher puffed up his cheeks round, poked at them with his fingers, and said, "It doesn't have this." When I thought about it later, I realized his gesture had a great meaning for me. Once, when I was washing the pavement in front of the gate with water from the faucet, a passerby said, "You Jap!" and made me feel very bad. At that time, too, when I looked in my teacher's eyes, I could forget everything.[2]

Later, when I took a night course in sculpture at an institute, Mr. Borglum happened to be the instructor. The institute gave us one compositional assignment a week, but I never responded, so he asked why. I had read somewhere that Tolstoy once said to Tokutomi Roka, "Don't write a novel unless you have the inner urge to do so," and so I quoted those words to him. He said, "That's good," and that was that. However, during the party at the end of the term he brought this story up and warned the students about art. He then offered his entire salary as a certain award.[3] Mr. Borglum was magnanimous, honest, pious, and natural. How I love and respect him! And I find it so encouraging that someone like him exists in the American art world. I do not doubt that he will one day contribute something valuable and significant to the art of the world. I will not say it will be a new school. It will be a man's true strength—and beauty.

Last year I received a report that Mr. Borglum is going to carve a gigantic monument on Mount Stone in Virginia. I expect that the plan is making progress. I'd like to end these old memories by quoting a passage from his recent letter:

"If you can, become a great sculptor. But it's even better to become a great human being and a loyal, good friend."

THE WORLD OF THE TACTILE

I am a sculptor.

Probably because of this, for me the whole world is tactile. The tactile sense is said to be the most primitive of the senses, but you can also say that it is therefore the most primordial. Sculpture is the most primordial art.

The "belly" of my ring finger perceives the rise and fall on the surface of a polished mirror. This is something I've recently discovered by accident, but the glass also has vertical and horizontal lines. If you close your eyes and caress the surface of ordinary glass, it feels just like the Satsuma wooden clog with neat grain. The surface of a polished mirror certainly can't be like a Satsuma wooden clog, but the "belly" of my finger knows that there are two waves even within a short span of five inches. This it perceives because it has the ability to perceive inclines. The sensation of feeling the waves on the surface of a mirror is comparable to that of feeling gentle pitching on board a ship. It's just so that it gives you a pleasant dizziness.

People speak of the five senses; but for me, the borderlines among those five senses aren't clear. They say the sky is blue. To that I'll say the sky is finely textured. They say the autumn clouds are white. White they are, yes, but they have the sort of sheen you get when you plane ginkgo wood diagonally, and are quite different from the puffy clouds in spring, which have the irregular veins of cypress wood from Kiso. When you think about it, it's quite natural that colors are tactile. The tremblings of lightwaves stimulate the retina purely in accordance with the principle of movement. The feeling of *tone* in painting, too, is tactile once you become aware of it. I can't say it well, but a painting with a *tone* has a certain tactile ineffability. A painting without it has fuzz like that of cotton thread that clings to the tip of your finger or is as painful as the heel that steps on a fragment of glass. If colors weren't tactile, we can well imagine that painted surfaces would feel eternally flattened out.

It will be unnecessary for me to repeat here that music is a tactile art. . . .

I'm told that smell consists of molecules. You smell manure, I'm told, because molecules from manure fly into you. That explains why I smell things with my skin. . . . Physiologically, too, the olfactory sense must be the tactile sense of the nasal membranes. So, without using associational adjectives, you can say there are voluminous smells, sandy smells, smooth smells, viscous smells, chatty smells, towering smells, and scorching smells.

The gustatory sense is of course tactile. Sweet, spicy, sour —these are all too general characterizations and cannot, in fact, be true concepts to measure tastes. The sweetness of mashed yam with chestnuts, for example, is a special kind of gustatory tactility peculiar to this food. It is not an extension of the sugar put into it.

Dry sugar is different from wet sugar. As commonly known, the Indians savor curried rice with their fingers, the afficionados of *soba* savor the noodles with their throats, and there are those who refuse to use chopsticks to eat sushi. Exquisite cooking lies in its *tone*. It's no different from the *tone* in colors.

It is not so much that the five senses share mutual commonality as that they are almost entirely unified by the tactile sense. The so-called sixth sense, i.e., the ability to sense relative positions, derives from the same root.[1] A sculptor can tell the horizontal position from the perpendicular while lying down. A carpenter measures columns and beams with a plumb bob and a square. A sculptor grasps them with the tactile sense of his eyes. Unless you know what the wind caused by a sword is like, you can't give form to your sculpture.

A sculptor has the tendency to want to grasp things. He has the tendency to want to see every phenomenon through the feeling he gets when he grasps it. To him, no phenomenon appears "picturesque." He caresses the moon to see what happens. He exposes himself to the sun the way he does to a bonfire. Trees, to be sure, stand individually. The ground, to be sure, is firmly there. No matter which part you look at, the landscape is subtly constructed. Like the human body it has a skeletal framework. It has muscles. It has skin. And it has proportions, it has organization. It has weight, it has lightness. It has what's explorable to the core.

Here's a poem. A sculptor even looks at life, as described here:

A certain man put his hand into Christ's chest to probe the two
    scars.
One stubborn sculptor
touches every phenomenon with his own fingers.
He tears the water apart to look inside,
cleaves heaven to get in there.
When he grabs you for certain, he thinks for the first time that
    you are you.

When a sculptor says he grabs you, he means to grab you naked. More often than not, we human beings don't know what each one of us looks like naked. We live clothed in excessive loads of things. A sculptor wants to take away all those accessories to see only your self. Take a man of erudition. His profound scholarship is not the man himself. His naked self lives deep inside, warm. Kant's philosophy is not Kant himself. He himself lives, as an individual being, deep

197

at the center of the axis that runs through his philosophy. Kuriyagawa Hakuson's scholarly knowledge is not himself. He himself exists as a separate being, crouched behind piles of books he has published. Sometimes a man, naked, is inseparable from his scholarship, and as great. Sometimes a man who reads admirably and behaves normally is, beneath his scholarship, a figure too horrible to behold.

Ordinarily, when people look at someone, they look at his distinguished career, his medals, his achievements, his talent, his thoughts, his assertions, his virtues, his temperament, or his personality. A sculptor first removes all of these. As long as there is something to be removed from the man, he robs him of the last shred. He then tries to grab what's left. Until he gets to that point, he doesn't think you are you. . . .

A sculptor's tactile sense tries to break through the mists [that shroud all phenomena]. . . .

Someone's life always has naked moments. Or, by switching the viewpoint, you can say any life is already naked as it is. But something made by human hands is not necessarily naked. It is delightful to look at some work made by human hands and touch the naked strength that exists in it. I do not refer to the strength of the way it is made, nor to that of its *tendency*. Both the way it is made and its tendency deserve full consideration. But in the end such considerations belong to a given period. The tactile sense that probes into the roots that are immovable begins to work first. Something that's on shaky ground about these roots or simply doesn't have them collapses when grabbed. Something that has them doesn't, no matter how feeble or shabby it may look. In poetry, Verlaine's lamentations don't collapse. Whitman's poetry, which is called nonpoetry, doesn't either. They will not, even when the time comes when the existence or nonexistence of such things doesn't matter. They will live even if they cease to be accepted. A work of art rooted in the maker's character, temperament, morality, thought, or talent won't last. Only that which stands on the roots you can't push or shove aside can give a firm response. Such a response renews your spirit. And this opens up thousands of different roads.

For me, the tactile sense is a terrible, fatal point.

MODERN JAPANESE
SCULPTURE

The world of Japanese sculpture since the Meiji Era has been extremely lacking in intelligence. That every one of the sculptors who taught at the Tokyo School of Fine Arts as seniors in sculpture during Meiji was a craftsman nurtured in the master-disciple tradition toward the end of the Tokugawa Period must have greatly influenced the Japanese sculpture that followed.

These people were all genuine, first-class Edo craftsmen. But a certain temperament they shared was communicated to those who followed them and held sway over the sculpture world. As a result, a society of sculptors came into being where skill rather than brain, or only skill, mattered, where no one dreamed of thinking about the nature of "sculpture itself," and where in the middle of narrow views and within small, terribly hidebound, partisan turfs they did nothing but hone their skills for a long time.

What these people made were not so much sculptures as crafts; indeed, in the early days their workplace was usually called *saikuba* ["craftsplace"]. Pieces carved out of wood were mainly intended, unless they were Buddhist statues, to be decorative pieces for alcoves, mirror frames to be hung on walls, and bas-reliefs for decorative partitions. Somewhat larger independent works were regarded as special pieces for exhibitions. Things like what constituted a sculpture never came into their thoughts. Ideals were like "a horse and a cow in heat together" or had no relevancy. They merely maintained part of the notion of sculpture through such concepts as *nikuai* ["fleshiness"] and *konashi* ["execution"] that were taught them in their training. But they were never aware of the roles these technical characteristics played in sculpture itself and what their limitations were. The value of a given piece was judged to be high or low merely on the basis of the sharpness of knife-cutting, the skill of execution, or the novelty of the idea given form.

And these people blindly protected, through guildlike banding together, the styles and ways of doing things of their own seniors—i.e., masters—and vied with one another in denigrating any other way of doing things. Someone who absorbed best his master's way of doing things was treated as the ranking disciple. The masters themselves maintained such total social control over their disciples that any disciple who went against his master had to be prepared to be deprived of even his right to make a living. Anyone who mouthed words like "art" was regarded as an intolerably fresh, foppish individual and usually ended up being crushed into a nonbeing. Such a milieu remained strong even until the period from the end of Meiji to early Taishō— the so-called period of the founding of the Bunten.

Meanwhile, the group of Western-style sculptors who received the guidance of foreign sculptors at the Engineering University[1] set the pattern of becoming contractors of Western-style architectural decorations and bronze statues and started building in parks and gardens a staggering number of extremely clumsy bronze statues that had no artistic basis.

Just about that time Ogiwara Morie, who had been converted by Rodin, returned from France, passionately talked about trends in European sculpture and the significance of Rodin, and himself submitted his works to the Bunten in his effort to enlighten Japanese sculptors. What he had to say was still loose and rough. Nevertheless he had a good impact on the sincere, young sculptors of the day and threw a gleam of light into the dark state of traditional sculpture. You can say that in the true sense of the term modern Japanese sculpture began with Ogiwara.

But, regrettably, before showing his full potential, he died young. And the sculpture world in general, which had not thought deeply of the meaning of his existence, again plunged into darkness. The sculptures of the Bunten became the standard for the whole generation, and the Bunten itself acquired the appearance of an extension of the Tokyo School of Fine Arts. It became, in effect, the exhibition place for works by the students of the school, and because of their leaders' incompetence, vulgar sculptures spread throughout Japan, thereby creating the general misunderstanding of sculpture. Even today a remnant of that tendency strongly endures.

TWO ASPECTS OF REALISM

As someone who from time to time makes *shasei* ["sketch-from-life"] styles of wood carving of such things as cicadas and pomegranates, I often feel sorely let down because even those who should know better show the shallowness of their understanding by saying to me things like, "This really looks as if it's flying" and "The way this pomegranate opens up, it looks like the real thing." In any such piece I have no intention of recreating the real thing as it is.

Among the portraits (Japanese-style paintings) at the Bunten some years ago was one that meticulously copied everything from real life—from the creases of the kimono the lady wore and the twists of the threads used in its fabric, to the printed characters in the newspaper she was reading. There is nothing as uninteresting as that kind of damnable *shasei*. In those days, "*shasei* sculptures" were also fashionable that tried to recreate apples, dried foods, and so forth in colossal detail, just as they actually look in real life.

Among the things that use the same type of *shasei* approach in crafts are the netsuke. A tobacco holder which, for example, is made to represent the shape of a hanging salted salmon would even try to recreate vividly the slack skin of the fish. These things are interesting in a certain way, but they are, in the end, not *sculptures*. Those who make them have no sculptural grasp of nature and objects (sculptural summation, sensibility). Where a round thing is simply presented as round, a thin thing as thin, there's no sculpture. A sculptor has, as part of his being, the *knack*—or the plastic sensibility—of making something thick but making it look thin, making something square but making it look round.

When such a person sketches from life, what he makes becomes by itself a sculpture.

In other words, I think there are two grades of *shasei*—low and high. A low grade of *shasei* is what ends up merely as copying life, and its only meaning is that it can be used as something you look up for comparison or as a record. Most of what are called *shasei* drawings or paintings today belong in this category; to me, they are like pictures for recording things or specimen illustrations used in textbooks, and have no independent value whatsoever. On the other hand, a high grade of *shasei* is not a mere record; just as life copied as it is in tanka and haiku can have symbolic import, so can life copied as it is in art have *mouvement, construction, composition*, and all the other ingredients that make up art. It isn't that when an artist sketches from life he gives attention to each such ingredient; but an artist, because he is one who has such factors in himself, can equip his sketch from life with them, thereby making a work of art effortlessly. If, however, someone who doesn't have them physically, temperamentally, tries to do the same, what he turns out, no matter what painstaking efforts he might make, will end up a mere record, material to be used for something else, or a detailed depiction. This is why I can't possibly believe that you can improve your art by simply devoting yourself to *shasei*.

Paintings of Hsuhsi,[1] such as one of lotuses, were probably meant to be pure sketches, their *compositions* not deliberate. Nevertheless, they reveal of necessity, along with other painterly ingredients, the plastic sensibility that Hsuhsi had as part of his physical ability; as a result, they greatly move you as works of art. Some years ago, however, when there was an exhibition of art from Sung, Yuan, Ming, and Ch'ing, there was a painting of lotuses by a painter, as I recall, from the Ming Dynasty. Interestingly enough, its composition was exactly the same as that of Hsuhsi's. Nonetheless, what it expressed looked shabby, and it couldn't be compared with Hsuhsi's painting. The difference was in innate ability—something you can't do anything about.

Though not a professional painter, Rodin has left us a number of interesting *dessins*, pencil drawings or lightly colored pencil drawings of figures. Many of these he did while following a moving model with his eyes, without looking at his drawing pad. At first he, too, did close sketches of ordinary models. But in 1900 he saw and took great interest in the dances of the Siamese court that were being performed at the World Fair in Paris and, frequently attending the performances, drew the dancers. (The *Rodin Monograph*, published in Germany, carries a photograph of Rodin drawing the Siamese dancers, in addition to reproductions of several drawings he did at the time.) It appears that he adopted the technique of keeping his eyes on his model from beginning to end about that time. He made his model move around the room as she pleased, and drew her at the moment of her falling, rising to her feet, or taking off her clothes. Because he drew them without looking at what his hands were doing, some of the lines fall on the same places and others veer off from one another without being linked properly. But because his lines were masterful, his drawings even have a suggestion of sensuality—a unique attractiveness rarely found in painters' drawings.

Rodin probably attempted this kind of drawing for research, in order to comprehend *mouvement*. Looking at the results, however, not only does *mouvement* appear in the rhythms of excellent lines, but the physicality and atmosphere are also acutely expressed in a fascinating manner. Rodin, then, is another example illustrating how someone with innate ability can make a work of art with independent value, which brings out what he has, even when he means to draw something innocuously.

The mind of an artist engaged in art is much simpler than might be expected, I've always thought. Once I referred to the late Natsume Sōseki's observation "Art begins in self-expression and ends in self-expression" and said, in a newspaper, "Art does not begin in self-expression; it simply begins in expression." In response, Mr. Natsume forwarded his complaint that I was unable to understand what philosophical speculation was. Thinking of myself engaged in art, I can't imagine my consciousness getting involved in the difficult task of expressing myself; when I'm carving someone's foot, I'm simply making a foot, but not doing it thinking any such thing as "I am expressing myself through this." . . . That was the impression I had, and I happened to say so by linking it to Mr. Natsume's sentence.

Of course, it is a fact that the artist himself sometimes contemplates his own art in the light of some theory of aesthetics or a theory of art, or analytically reflects on the mentality or motive of his work. But once he begins to work, he returns to something unexpectedly innocuous and infantile, and, in most cases I think, starts with a thought no more portentous than that of copying real life. And even when he is, say, painting independently of *shasei* intentions, it seems to me that he doesn't mean to alter willfully, drastically, what he has received from nature, but to maintain, at heart, the innocuous desire to leave it as it is, carefully.

In that process, the sum of the plastic things that the artist (not only understands but also) has as part of himself becomes *realisé* in his work inevitably and individually, as I've said before. It follows that what is called *shasei* here doesn't mean mere copying, drawing something as it is in real life.

In this sense, paintings such as the *Fuji* (Kiyomi Temple) and the *Sansui-zu chōkan* by Sesshū, the "single-stroke drawings" by the swordsman Miyamoto Musashi, and the "splattered-ink" figure drawings by Liangkai[2] came into being, I don't think, independently of *shasei*. Ike no Taiga, too, studied nature by visiting various places and thus started out from a sort of *shasei*. I think that, generally, things with this approach at their base make authentic, deep-rooted, layered art. There have always been landscape paintings that are deliberately out of the boundary of *shasei*, products that are purely off the top of the head, but they are weak in some unaccountable ways, overwhelmed as they are —you can't deny—by points that immediately "attract" or "appeal to" you. Some of them occasionally move you, but they are nonetheless on the side roads.

Michelangelo is an artist who rebelled throughout his career against the notion of copying real life. He insisted on the idealized forms modeled on classical Greek beauty, although the insistence was at the same time an attempt to defy and transcend the narrow literalism of Donatello, an Italian artist like him but living a century earlier. The actual impression you get from the latter's statue, *St. John the Baptist in a Fur,* is no different from that you may get of an old beggar. As an attempt to copy life, it's very real indeed, and its execution is highly skillful. As a portrait sculptor, he must be the best in history. But his sculptures give to the human spirit something petty and shabby. Michelangelo, who found Donatello's approach lacking, insisted that he would not make any portrait sculpture. Here again, though, the difference between the two was a matter of temperament; anything as shabby as Donetallo's works could not possibly have come from Michelangelo's hands.

From Michelangelo's works—such as the sculptures on the

wall-tombs in San Lorenzo that he sculpted for Lorenzo di Medici (a statue of Lorenzo in his robes at the center and, beneath it, sculptures of two nudes, male and female, called *Dawn* and *Evening*, contrastingly placed)—we are made to understand what the human body is exactly like, without knowing an actual human body. And yet they show the artist's close observation of details, though the details as a whole are wrapped in something larger. From our viewpoint, he was copying from life. It would be unthinkable to avoid *shasei* and still create that kind of art.

A certain German book[3] even shows photographs of people striking the poses of Michelangelo's figures on these wall-tombs of the Medici to contrast them with his sculptures. But even without comparing them with Michelangelo's bodies, which express the essence of the human body with a terrifying artistic power, the human bodies shown in the photographs are so shabby as to force you to avert your eyes. When you think of it, you can't help wondering how different the bronze statues standing in various parts of Tokyo are from those figures in the photographs. To me, most of them look as though the three-dimensional photos I recently saw at a Shiseidō exhibition were put on pedestals.

In sum, what I'm trying to say is extremely simple. What I've said in a leisurely fashion may be summarized as follows.

If someone who is equipped with the essence of art or an artistic sense, someone who has it physically, does *shasei*, there will be some meaning in it; but if someone who doesn't have it does *shasei*, he can't help turning out in the end what will only be a record.

The relationship between *shasei* and art may also be considered from the following two aspects:

1. Art doesn't move forward as long as it sticks to *shasei*.
2. Authentic art can't be born where there is no *shasei*.

THE BEAUTY AND THE
PLASTICITY OF THE
CICADA

I often carve a cicada out of wood. No bird, animal, insect, or fish is outside my interest, but from the viewpoint of plastic arts, some are appropriate for sculpting, and some not. I have many friends among insects, and grasshoppers, crickets, dragonflies, praying mantises, cicadas, and spiders are among my close friends. In particular I have a great attachment to the mantis with his triangular head, and often pull a strand of hair from my head and feed it to him. The mantis loves human hair and can devour any number of strands of it as long as you keep presenting them to him. His character, which doesn't have any sense of fear, is fascinating, too. But you can't make a sculpture out of him. His shape isn't good for sculpture. The grasshopper and the cricket are also useless in this regard. Among the dragonflies, there are the statuesque ones like the *gin'yamma*, flimsy ones like the *tōsumitombo*, and prettily decked-out ones like the *akatombo*, so they may look interesting for sculpture; but they, too, are no good. They give little sculptural impetus. If you try, you can make a sculpture out of them, but if you do, you damage the beauty and dignity of nature and end up making not a sculpture but a toy, or something to be treasured by literati. In this regard, the cicada is quite different. He comes with something terribly sculptural in his form. In addition, I have, of course, loved him since well before I became involved in sculpture.

Children all love this living concertina. When I was a child, I too ran around in the woods of Yanaka Tennōji in the summer to catch him. You peel the bark off an ilex and mash it with a stone to make strong bird-lime. Even now I remember, somewhat sentimentally, the joy of licking my fingers to roll the lime around the tip of a bamboo pole. For some reason, I didn't know in those days the method of collecting spiderwebs to catch the cicada. I've learned about it recently. If you can catch him that way, that ought to be better. That probably won't damage his wings. Whenever I unexpectedly discovered a cicada perched on the trunk of a low tree, rasping, I used to become so excited that my heart would begin to beat. I still do.

On summer evenings I sometimes go out to hunt for models, but in most cases I can't catch them myself but come home with some given me by the children I know. When I see a cicada intently rasping as if trying to squeeze the last drop of sound out of himself, he looks so very serious as to make me hesitate to catch him. Once he stops rasping, he immediately flies up and, after bumping into surrounding things in his hastiness, settles on a new spot and resumes his rasping as if he didn't have a single moment to waste. I can't help sympathizing with that single-mindedness of his in calling for love. He's so obsessed with his rasping that it's as if, in his intentness in calling, he had forgotten what the purpose of his calls was. In fact, I have never seen a cicada who has won his mate.

In Tokyo there seem to be at most the *jīji*, *abura*, *minmin*, *tsukudukubōshi*, and *kanakana*, but not the *haruzemi*, *chitsuchizemi*, *kumazemi*, and *ezozemi*. For this reason, the number of species I have actually held in my hand is extremely small; among others, I have yet to see the *haruzemi* and *ezozemi*. As for the *kumazemi*, I saw one some years ago, in Atami, perched at the top of a pine tree and rasping, but I couldn't reach it with my pole, so couldn't get hold of it. The *jījī* is the most rustic-simple; with his eyes wide apart, it looks as if he's feigning dumbness. The *abura* is large, sharp, barbarous, and tough, and, as might be expected from his overwhelming voice, which is unstoppable and continuous, and ever *fortissimo*, he's also built to be simply, straightforwardly, a powerhouse. I love to make this cicada. That his wings are untransparent and dark brown, his body relatively long, and his head small, is also good for sculpture.

In comparison, the *minmin* looks gorgeous, beauteous, technically well made, and superior in quality. With his wings transparent, the green and black designs on his chest and belly intriguing, he comes out loud in sculpture. His body is short, and the way his belly suddenly shrinks at its tip is amusing. In sculpture you inlay mica or rub silver dust on his wings. The *tsukutsukubōshi* and *kanakana* are feminine and die as soon as you catch them. They also look delicate, elegant, and carry the feeling which some pale-blue spirits might. The *kumazemi*, also known as the *shanshan*, is the giant among the cicadas; in addition to black and green, he has orange blended into his body, and his wings are transparent, powerful, and shapely—or so I hear, but I have never seen him in my own hand, so I don't know him in detail. As for the *haruzemi*, I heard his subdued, mysterious voice in a pinewood on Mount Yūkyū, in Nagaoka, Echigo, toward the end of May some years ago, but I couldn't see him.

The sculptural impetus of the cicada lies in the way his whole body is put together nicely. The details are complex, but they are unified by his two large wings. Further, the relationship between the protrusions of the compound eyes at the two edges of his head and his chest is not fragile. His chest is as strong as armor, and the design on the wrinkled bag at the end of the back of his mid-chest has a particularly interesting sculptural form and mass. The back of his belly is encased neatly in his wings. His six limbs are not too long, and his forelimbs make strong arms. His mouth is also unimaginably well proportioned, with a sucking beak at its center. On the whole, the cicada is easy to simplify and has no wasteful planes.

The subtlest part of the cicada's beauty lies in the mountain-shaped line his wings make when you look at him from his side. A semiroundness is formed from his head to the back of his chest, where the upper rim of his wing rises upward and then, after forming a peak, goes down again in waves as if avalanching and ends, after rising up for a moment. This is the line unique to the cicada, not seen in anything else. The contrast between this wavy shape of the upper rim of the wing and the simple curve of its lower rim is beautiful. You may say it is the ultimate of the linear beauty that the cicada has. Each species of cicada has its own special proportion of these wavy patterns.

The beauty of the cicada's wings is wonderful even when you look at them not from the side but from above. The two wings on the right and on the left are balanced well. The outer outline delineates a slow but strong curve and runs away to the farthest end; inside, the lines are drawn as if two wavy shapes are brought together from left and right, which in the lower half open up again before tightening up a little at the very end.

The cicada doesn't change his shape much whether alive or dead, but the tips of his wings are an exception. When he's alive, the tips slightly close inward; when dead, they're left open. Needless to say, it's more beautiful when they're slightly closed.

In wood carving, whether or not the sculpted piece turns

out to be interesting will depend on the way the thin wings are carved. If you carve them thin the way they are, you'll make them vulgar, coarse, and as hard as tin, and will in the end lose sculpturalness. You must deal with this problem by interpreting the meaning of wings through the delicate question of mass and by following the feeling of the wood you use. Most of the cicadas carved in metal look vulgar because this is not considered. It's thoughtless to make every thin thing as thin as it actually is. You can make it about double the original size. This is true not only in wood carving, but in sculpture in general, in art in general. A poem which blindly brings an emotion to the surface does not necessarily convey it, but can be coarse and *dull*; meanwhile, an expression in the opposite direction can bring out a strong emotion.

This doesn't mean you can simply carve the cicada wings thick; if you do that, they'll look bloated and stupid, because what you've made will be a cicada in a padded gown. To make the wings thick but not to give a thick feeling—this can be done in sculpture only by handling the mass and planes well. Furthermore, the finished sculpture should come to your eyes as smoothly as if such questions didn't exist, in a way that will not make you aware whether the wings are thick or thin. The best piece will be the one that makes you feel that's the way it's made. This is beauty. It's because, in this instance, the sculptor is not making *what looks like a cicada* but sculpting a plastic beauty based on a cicada. It is because of this that the sculptor must be someone who has carried out a strict scientific study of the form of the cicada and fully understood the principles of the way it is constructed. Without that detailed knowledge, he wouldn't be able to explore its plasticity with a peaceful mind. As long as he feels careless about it or doesn't mind

213

just guessing things, he can't attain a structural freedom. Unless you are free while at the same time on a firm basis, you can't create a true beauty.

Just as the Egyptians loved to carve the scarabaeus, their symbol of eternal life, for talismen, so the ancient Greeks made small carvings of cicadas as a symbol of beauty, happiness, and peace, and used them for decorations, such as accessories. We're told that they adored the cicadas' rasps and harmonious beauty. In Japan cicadas are generally thought to be noisy, and the *abura*, among others, is regarded as representative of the things that make the sultry summer even sultrier. It may be that in Greece, where there aren't too many trees, the cicadas' rasps are much quieter. Or perhaps their cicadas are like our *kanakana*.

Either way, to me, the way the Japanese cicadas rasp as loudly as they can, with childlike abandon, the way their rasps pierce the core of my brain, is very pleasant. Indeed, what's described as *semi shigure*, "cicada shower," or the competitive performance of cicadas in the woods, is a gift of the summer, as beautiful as a dream. When I carve a cicada, I feel as if a breeze dripping with the green of such woods fills my room.

THE LATTER HALF OF
CHIEKO'S LIFE

In ten days it will be fully two years since my wife, Chieko, died of miliary tuberculosis while a schizophrenic patient in Room 15 of James-zaka Hospital, in Minami-Shinagawa. Because I encountered Chieko, I had the experience of being cleansed by her pure love and rescued from my earlier decadent life, and because my spirit lay solely in her very existence, the spiritual blow from her death was severe indeed, and, for a while feeling as if I had lost the goal of my art as well, I spent months possessed by a sense of emptiness.

When she was alive, I would first show her each sculpture I made before showing it to anybody else. At the end of work each day, too, nothing gave me greater joy than to examine with her what I had done. She, for her part, wholly accepted my work, understood it, loved it passionately. She so loved the small wooden pieces I made that she would lovingly carry them in the bosom of her kimono when she walked in the town. In the world where she's no more, who will accept my sculptures like a child? The thought that there was no longer anyone to whom I could show them troubled me for months. Work related to beauty can never come into being out of an official principle or a grand national awareness alone. Such things may become the theme for your work or the motive for it, but for the work to come from the bottom of your heart and acquire living blood, an exchange of great love is absolutely needed. At times it can be the love of God. At times it can be the love of the Sovereign. At times it can also be the bottomless purity of one woman's love. Nothing gives more strength to an artist than the consciousness that there is one person who will look at what he makes with passionate love. Nothing gives him a stronger latent power to finish making at any cost what he wants to make. The result of his work may benefit all the people. But in his heart the artist always wants just one such person to look at what he's made. I had such a person in my wife, Chieko. The sense of emptiness immediately after she died was therefore almost like the world of nothingness. I had many things I wanted to make but didn't feel like making them. Because I knew the eyes that would look at them with passionate love had now ceased to exist in this world.

After struggling like that for several months, as a result of a coincidence, one moonlit night I had the acute sense that Chieko had become a universal being for me by losing her individual being. After that I could always feel her breath close; she became, let's say, the one with whom I existed, and the sense became strong that she was eternal to me. Thus I recovered my ordinary mind and health, and the incentive for work revived again. When I finish a day's work, look at what I've done, and turn back and say, "What do you think?" Chieko is there at once. She is everywhere.

Chieko's life during the twenty-four years between marriage and death was simply an uninterrupted sequence of love, difficult daily living, hard work devoted to art, contradictions, and struggles with illness. In the midst of such a vortex she fell because of the mental quality she was fated to have, and sank away in the waves entangled with bliss, despair, trust, and resignation. Urged by people a number of times to write my memories of her, I didn't feel like doing so until today. After such raw, painful struggles, I couldn't bear to pen even one tiny corner of our life; also, the doubt that there could be any meaning in a report on what was no more than a private life strongly restrained my mind.

But now I will write. I will write down the fate of this one woman as simply as I can. By writing for the record that during the eras of Taishō and Shōwa there was a woman who suffered, lived, and fell the way she did, I will ask her to permit me to make a farewell gift for her, that pitiful soul. Believing that what is true of one person applies to thousands of others, I dare take up my pen to write this, in spite of the times such as they are today.

As I calmly look back and reflect on her now, her life may be summarized as follows.

First, she was born in the nineteenth year of Meiji the first daughter of the Naganuma family, a sake brewer in a place called Urushibara, near Nihonmatsu-chō, Fukushima Prefecture, in the Tōhoku Region. After graduating from a local girls' high school, she entered the home economics department of Japan Women's College, in Mejiro, Tokyo. While continuing her dormitory life, she began to have an interest in Western-style painting. After graduation from college, she stayed in Tokyo, obtaining extremely reluctant agreement from her parents in her hometown, and attended the Pacific Western-style Painting Institute to study oil painting. She associated with such rising painters of the day as Nakamura Tsune, Saitō Yoriji, and Tsuda Seifū, and was influenced by them; she also joined the women's thought movement proposed by Hiratsuka Raichō and others about the same time, and did some cover paintings for the magazine *Seitō* [Blue Stockings].

That was in the last years of Meiji. Not long afterward she came to know me through the introduction of Yanagi Yaeko and married me in the third year of Taishō. After marriage, too, she was passionately devoted to oil painting. But the days when she had to struggle between concentration on art and daily life increased. Besides, after she suffered from pleurisy, she was often forced to take to her bed. Later, her father back home died, which was followed by the bankruptcy of the family; all this gave her an inordinate amount of pain and worry. Soon, as a result of mental irregularities caused by menopause, she began to have symptoms of psychological problems. In the seventh year of Shōwa she attempted suicide with adaline. Fortunately, she could get away from this medicinal poison and regained her health for a while. But, after that, because of the disorder of her brain cells that pushed away all sorts of treatment and slowly but steadily moved forward, she was, in the tenth year of Shōwa, totally gripped by schizophrenia. In February of the same year, she was admitted to James-zaka Hospital, and there, in October of the thirteenth year of Shōwa, quietly closed her eyes forever.

Chieko's life was extremely simple, and began and ended as one privately lived, which hardly touched any activity with social import. If you were to seek any time when she had social contact, you could only point to the brief period when she was involved with *Seitō*. She not only had few social concerns; she was by nature not sociable. While involved with *Seitō*, she was rather well-known among a certain group of people as one of the so-called new women, and the name Naganuma Chieko was sometimes bandied about in their conversations. But this came about because those fond of gossiping in those days spread fancy stories about her in an amusing fashion; it appears that she herself was laconic, unsociable, and illogical, and went about her business in her own single-minded way. It seems that her woman friends' true opinion was, "It's difficult to talk to Miss Naganuma."

I don't know much about her from those days, but I remember reading in a piece Mr. Tsuda Seifū wrote somewhere that he often saw her walking in high, lacquered wooden clogs and looking as though she were dragging the lower hem of her kimono. Such an appearance and the fact that she talked little made people see, I think, some sort of curious mystery in her. It seems that she was thought to be someone out of the *Female Water Margin*, or said to be fond of fashionable things, but I imagine that in reality she was innocuous and indifferent.

I should say I know practically nothing about the first half of Chieko's life. What I know about her is limited to the period after I was introduced and became acquainted with her. I was up to my neck with things of the moment, so didn't have any inclination to learn what had gone before. I didn't even know her exact age until years later.

The Chieko I came to know had an extremely simple and sincere personality. With her heart always brimming with something celestial, she seemed a woman who exposed her entire self to love and trust. Born to dislike losing, she seemed to keep her emotions to herself to quite a degree. She acted mild-mannered and didn't show any light-headedness. At times the strength of her willpower to surpass herself and move forward surprised me; but behind it, I surmise in retrospect today, lay a great deal of strenuous effort that was revealed to no one.

I didn't realize it at the time, but when I thought about it later, the second half of her life seemed, in the end, to have proceeded in a way that would lead to mental illness. It seems that, living with me, she had no other path to take. Before trying to think why this was so, I imagine a different life for her and wonder what it might have been like if, for example, she had lived, not in Tokyo, but in her hometown or on some farm, her spouse not an artist like me but of some other profession with an understanding of art, especially someone engaged in tilling the land and raising cattle. In that case, she might have lived out her natural span of years.

This possibility is compelling because Tokyo was physically so unsuited to her. For her, the air of Tokyo was always tasteless, dry, and gritty. Urged by President Naruse, of the Women's College, she rode a bicycle, became passionate about tennis, and seems to have spent a very healthy, active youth. After graduation, however, she couldn't be said to be strong on the whole, but looked willowy, and it appears that she spent nearly half of each year in the countryside or in the mountains. After she began to live with me, too, she would return to her hometown for three or four months a year. Without breathing the air of the countryside, her body couldn't last. She often lamented, "There's no sky in Tokyo." Here's my short poem called "Child's Talk":

Chieko says Tokyo has no sky at all,
says she wants to see the real sky.
Surprised, I look at the sky:
there among fresh cherry leaves
is a familiar, clear sky that I can't separate from.
The dull, smoldering haze at the horizon
is the pink moist of the morning.
Looking far off Chieko says:
The blue sky that every day comes out
above Mount Atatara is
the real sky I mean.
This is just child's talk of the sky.

Because I myself was born and raised in Tokyo, I couldn't feel her painful appeal as my own, thinking she would eventually become used to the nature of this city. But her demand for a fresh, transparent nature never changed until her life was ended. While in Tokyo she tried to fill this demand in various ways. She tirelessly sketched the weeds growing around our house, studied them botanically, cultivated lilies and tomatoes in the bay window, ate vegetables raw, indulged herself by listening to a record of Beethoven's Sixth Symphony—all such things must have been variations on her attempt to fulfill that demand. This one fact alone

220

suggests that her inexpressible, uninterrupted pain spanning half her life was more than can be imagined. On her last day, her joy several hours before death, when she held a Sunkist lemon in her hand that I had brought her, must have also been part of this. When she bit into that lemon, she looked as if both her body and soul were being washed in its refreshing fragrance and juice.

The greater reason that she ended with a mental collapse must have been her suffering from the contradictions and dead ends that arose between her fierce concentration on art, above all else, and her attempt to live a daily life founded on pure love for me. She passionately loved painting. It seems that already at the Women's College she had begun to paint in oils, and I'm told that at the students' festivals she would always take on the job of painting the backdrops for plays. I've also heard that even though they had initially objected, her parents finally agreed to her plan to become a painter because the skill apparent in a portrait she did of her grandfather about that time astonished the people of her hometown. This painting I saw later. While innocuous, it had a subdued harmony, a work beautiful in its color values.

I don't know much about the paintings she did during the several years after her graduation, but I think they probably were somewhat mood-oriented, with sweet feelings. She destroyed all the works from those days, never showing them to me. I can only imagine what they were like from some sketches and first drafts.

After we began to live together, she mainly studied still life and did hundreds of paintings. She painted landscapes when she went back to her hometown or traveled to the mountains. As for figures, she did drawings, but ended up not doing them in oils in a serious manner. She was devoted to Cezanne and, naturally, was strongly influenced by him.

In those days I too did oil painting, in addition to sculpture, but we had separate rooms for our work. Chieko struggled very hard with colors, and suffered. And because she did not desire any halfway success, she blamed herself almost to the point of self-torture. One year, she spent the summer at Goshiki Hot Springs near her hometown and came back with paintings of the landscapes there. Some of the small pieces among them were rather good, and she was persuaded to submit them to the Bunten. So we carried them in, along with one large piece; but the judges saw no merit in them, and they were all rejected. After that, no matter how much I encouraged her, she wouldn't submit any work of hers for any exhibition anywhere. For any artist to have an opportunity to exhibit his work in public, thereby bringing out his pent-up feelings for the world to see and dispersing them is, I think, a form of psychological help. But Chieko, by shutting up her own self forever because of that rejection, may have worsened her introversive tendencies.

Because she aimed only for the best, she was always dissatisfied with herself, and her work always ended up unfinished. True, I can't argue the fact that some of her oil paintings were inadequate in color. She showed wonderful power and elegance in her drawings, but she was unable as yet to master oil paint adequately, though she tried. She sorrowed over this. Sometimes I found her alone in tears in front of her canvas. When I happened to go to her room on the second floor and found her in that state, I often felt an undescribable loneliness and could not bring myself to say consoling words.

Incidentally, I was far shorter of the means of livelihood than people may imagine. We had a maid only once, around the time of the Great Earthquake. For the rest of our life we lived by ourselves. And because both Chieko and I were similar plastic artists, we had considerable difficulty juggling our time. Once we became absorbed in work, neither of us could have a meal, clean the house, and run errands throughout the day, every aspect of daily life coming to a standstill. As such days accumulated, in the end Chieko, as a woman, had to handle domestic chores after all. Worse, as the number of occasions became frequent when I had to work on sculpture during the day and write articles at night, scarcely sparing time for supper, more and more of her time for studying painting was eaten away. If the work is writing poetry, half of it can be done in your head, so you can make use of rather small time slots. But when it comes to plastic arts, you can't do anything without certain blocks of time. So I could well imagine Chieko's pain and worries. She struggled so hard not to reduce the time for my work, no matter what, to protect my sculpture, to fend chores off from me. Before long she had reduced the amount of time for her own study of painting and begun to try her hand at sculpting in clay and, later, spinning silk threads, trying plant dyes on them, or weaving. The kimono and haori she made by her own hand are still with me. Mr. Yamazaki Hin, an authority on plant dyes, wrote a tanka and cabled it when she died:

> Weaving a streak of blue into the sleeves
> that elegant person's now no more.

Although to the end she didn't say it, she had despaired of her work in oil painting. For her to give up this field of art, which she considered her life's work, could not have been mentally easy. In a later year, the night she took poison, there was in the next room a basket full of fruit, just purchased and brought home from Senbiki-ya, arranged in a manner appropriate for still-life painting, and an easel with a fresh canvas on it. When I saw it, I felt as if stabbed in the chest. I felt like wailing.

Because she was gentle but disliked losing, she kept everything to herself and went ahead quietly. And she always poured her best abilities into everything. In things related to art, yes, in matters of general knowledge or in psychological matters, she thought through everything, didn't tolerate ambiguity, and despised compromises. In a way, she was like a string kept taut twenty-four hours a day. Unable to bear that tension, her brain cells broke. She became exhausted, and fell.

I don't know how often I felt cleansed by the cleanliness of her inner life. Compared with her, I felt entirely aimless and muddled. Just looking at her eyes, I always received a hundred lessons. In her eyes there certainly was that heavenly sky above Mount Atatara. When I made a bust of her, I felt keenly that those eyes were out of my reach and was ashamed how dirty I was. Even when I think of it now, it seems that she kept as part of her inner self the fate of not being able to live safely in this world. So isolatedly did she live in a world whose air was different from that of this world.

I remember feeling at times that she was somehow a spirit temporarily existing in this world. She had none of the worldly desires. She lived single-mindedly for art and for love of me. And she was always young. She was not only young in spirit but remarkably young in her looks. When I traveled with her, no matter where we went, people thought she was my younger sister, or even thought she was my daughter. She had somehow that kind of youthfulness. Even near her death, she didn't look like a woman over fifty years old. About the time of our marriage, I couldn't imagine her in old age, so I said jokingly, "I wonder if you'll ever become an old woman." As I recall, she unthinkingly responded to this by saying, "I'll die before getting old." This is exactly what happened.

In the opinions of psychiatrists, the brains of ordinary healthy people can put up with a considerable degree of anxiety, and most of those who suffer from mental illness are either born with it, in one form or another, or come to have it after birth by injury or serious disease. Chieko didn't seem to have anyone who was mentally ill in her genealogy. Except that her younger brother, the first son of her family, behaved in a manner considerably out of the ordinary, and because of that her family went bankrupt and he himself contracted a dreadful disease and died poverty-stricken, in a miserable place. But I can't believe that there flowed between the two a current of traits that can be termed hereditary. I'm also told that in childhood she sustained a terrible injury to her skull from a cut stone; but it later healed completely, without causing any trouble, and I can't think it had anything to do with the illness she had in her later years.

Also, when she developed irregularities in her brain, her doctor asked me if I hadn't been infected with a certain disease in a foreign country. I didn't have any recollection of any such thing. Furthermore, Chieko and I had our blood tested time and again, but the result was always negative. From all this, it is hard to decide that the characteristics that might have caused her illness called schizophrenia had existed physically in her.

But then, when I think of it in retrospect, I can also see that all the tendencies of hers after I knew her made their way, slow step by slow step, toward that illness. Even her pure-mindedness had something extraordinary about it. Once she drove herself to a resolve, she would give up everything else and have no regrets. Hers was, in short, the sort of temperament that, as the saying goes, "no arrows or shields could stop." The strength and depth of her love for and trust in me was, I dare say, that of an infant. What struck me first

225

about her, indeed, was the abnormal beauty of her character. If I may say so, she was abnormal in every way. It was because of this feeling I had that I sang, in my poem called "Two under the Tree,"

> This is where you were born,
> the heaven and earth that gave birth to your mysterious unique
> flesh.

Whether she reached her last collapse step by step or the illness, turning like a spiral, pushed toward her inexorably, it was only toward the end that I began to notice for the first time, though in no clear manner, that something about her was odd. Until then I had not had a smidgen of doubt about her mental state. In other words, she was abnormal, but she wasn't. I felt her abnormality distinctly for the first time when she was close to menopause.

I will simply write down what I remember about her.

As I said before, it was Yanagi Yaeko, Chieko's senior graduate of the Women's College, who introduced her to me. Miss Yanagi was the wife of the painter Yanagi Keisuke, whom I had known since my New York days and was at the time working for the Ōfū-kai [Cherry-Maple Club]. It was the forty-fourth year of Meiji. I had returned from France in July of the forty-second year of Meiji and, turning my father's retirement hut in his garden into a studio by making a hole in its roof, was actively pursuing sculpture and oil painting there. I had also started a small gallery called Rōkan-dō in Awaji-chō, Kanda, where I held shows for the "New Movement Art." At the same time, I had joined the Subaru group's new literary movement that had erupted in Japan then, and, my delayed youth exploding, I was indulging rather fiercely in the so-called decadent life, in the frequent companionship of Kitahara Hakushū, Nagata Hideo,

Kinoshita Mokutarō, and others. Because of anxieties, irritability, thirst, and despair about something unidentified, I was leading an awfully messed up life. I had schemed to migrate to Hokkaidō, and failed in no time. It was when I was experiencing a mental crisis whose outcome I myself couldn't tell.

Just about that time, perhaps because Mr. Yanagi as a friend gave deep thought to the matter, Chieko was introduced to me. She was terribly elegant, laconic, and, when she spoke, her sentences would fade away toward the end. She would just look at my work, drink tea, hear me talk about French painting, and go home. At first, I didn't notice anything other than the way she knew how to dress smartly and the impression she gave with her delicate appearance. Because she never brought me any of the paintings she did, I knew nothing about the sorts of things she painted.

Not long afterward, my father built me my present atelier. It was completed in the forty-fifth year of Meiji, and I moved in here, alone. Chieko came to visit with a large pot of gloxinia to celebrate the occasion.

Just after the death of Emperor Meiji, I went to Inubō to do some drawing. Chieko had come to stay in a different inn with her younger sister and a close friend of hers, so I met her again. Later, she came to stay in my inn, and the two of us took walks, had meals, went out to draw. We must have looked strange: every time we took a walk, one of the maids of the inn would invariably follow us to watch. It appears that they thought we might commit double suicide. According to what Chieko told me at a later date, she was determined to go into the water and die if I said anything that went against her will in any way. I wasn't aware that she had any such intent, but I was strongly impressed by the purity of attitude, her nonacquisitive, innocuous character, and boundless love of nature. The way she expressed delight at the beach windbreak on Kimigahama, she was just like a child. But at the same time, when I was taking a bath and accidentally saw her in the next bathing room, I had the sudden premonition that the two of us might be linked by fate. She had such a well-proportioned body.

Soon her passionate letters began to arrive, and I myself came to feel that there was no other person to whom I could commit my heart. Still, I often doubted if my feelings were not temporary. I also warned her about this. That was because when I thought of the painful struggles ahead to make a living, I couldn't bear involving her in all that. About that time malicious gossip about us was thrown about among a small circle of artists and women, and both of us felt terribly awkward in relation to our families. But Chieko was unswerving in her trust in me, and I revered her for that. The more malicious voices rose around us, the more firmly we were united. Because I knew the impure elements and muddled dregs that were in me, I was often about to lose self-confidence, but each time she illuminated what was in me in clear light. This is why I sang:

> In the various soiled figures that I'd become,
> with infant truthfulness
> you found my noble self.
> What you found is strange to me
> but, because I consider you a supreme judge,
> relying on you I rejoice in my heart
> and believe that what is hidden in my warm flesh
> is the self I do not know.

It was Chieko's pure, single-minded love that finally pulled me out of my go-for-broke mood of decadence and saved me.

For the two months of August and September in the second year of Taishō, I stayed at Shimizu-ya in Kamikōchi, Shinshū, and made fifty to sixty oil paintings for Seikatsu-sha's exhibition that I held with Kishida Ryūsei, Kimura Sōhachi, and others at the Venus Club in Kanda that fall. In those days anybody who wanted to go to Kamikōchi used to start from Shimajima, go through Iwanadome, and over Tokugō Pass; it was quite a distance. During that summer, staying in the same inn were Kubota Utsubo and Ibaragi Inokichi, as well as Mr. and Mrs. Weston who had just come to climb Hodaka. As September began, Chieko came to visit me with painting materials. When notified of this, I went over Tokugō Pass to meet her at Iwanadome. Leaving her luggage to her guide, she had climbed lightly dressed. The mountain people were surprised at what a good walker she was. I guided her, again crossing Tokugō Pass, this time with her, to Shimizu-ya.

Her joy at the scenery in Kamikōchi was great. From then on we walked around, making drawings, with me carrying our art supplies on my shoulders. At the time she appeared to have some minor problem with her pleurae, but while on the mountains it didn't develop into anything serious.

It was then that I saw her paintings for the first time. She had a considerably subjective view of nature that was in a way unique, and I thought that it would be interesting if she grew to be great. I painted everything I observed: Hodaka, Myōjin, Yaketake, Kasumizawa, Roppyakutake, the Azusa River. Even in her sickbed in later years Chieko would look at one of the self-portraits I did at the time.

Once the Westons asked me if Chieko was my younger sister or my wife. When I said she was a friend of mine, they smiled with some incredulity. About that time, with the headline "Love on the Mountain," a newspaper in Tokyo wrote with exaggeration about the two of us in Kamikōchi.

It had probably expanded on a rumor from someone who had gone down the mountain. The article again grated on the nerves of our families.

On the first of October all of us on the mountain went down to Shimajima. The magnificence of the yellow leaves of the katsura trees that filled the bosom of the mountain at Tokugō Pass was unforgettable. Chieko, too, often recalled it and talked about it.

From then on my parents were terribly worried. I felt very sorry for my mother. All the dreams of both father and mother were shattered. I wouldn't take advantage of the position of someone who "had returned from the West" to push myself into the sculpture world, I declined to become a schoolteacher though that was urged, I didn't take an appropriate Edo bride—all of which confused them about my intentions. Though I felt very sorry, in the end, in the third year of Taishō, I asked my parents to allow me to marry Chieko. They did. As that meant I couldn't serve them but would live separately in my atelier, we arranged that all their house, land, and other effects be owned by my younger brother and his wife, who lived with them. The two of us, Chieko and I, set up a household, entirely bare, so to speak. Needless to say, we didn't go to Atami for a honeymoon. After that, for a very long stretch of time we lived in poverty.

Chieko was brought up in a prosperous family, but, perhaps because of that, she was quite indifferent to money matters and did not know the horrors of poverty. When I ran out of money and called in a used-clothes dealer to sell my suits, she looked on untroubled, and when there was no money in the drawer for household accounts, she simply didn't go out shopping. Sometimes we wondered aloud, "Suppose the time comes when we can't eat any more." But if I said, "Well, no matter what may happen, we've got to do all the work we have to," she would often say, "You're right, we should never allow your sculpture to fade somewhere along the way." We didn't have a fixed income, but when we had money, we had a good deal of it, and when we didn't, we had absolutely nothing for the next day. If you run out of money, you can't find it no matter where you may look. During our twenty-four years together I probably managed to buy her a kimono only two or three times. She gradually ceased to wear the flashy kimonos from her unmarried days, became in the end unadorned, and came to wear nothing other than a sweater and trousers around the house. And in them she struck an exceptionally beautiful harmony. It was in those days that, in a poem called "You Gradually Become More Beautiful," I wrote:

As a woman gradually discards her accessories
why does she become so beautiful?
Your body, washed with age,
is heaven's metal flying through infinity.

Though never alarmed by her own poverty, Chieko was greatly pained by the collapse of her family. She went back to her family several times to try to put, it seems, their household accounts in order, but in the end the family went bankrupt. A great fire in Nihonmatsu-chō. Her father's death. The inheritor's licentious behavior. Bankruptcy. These things must have been matters of great regret unbearable for her. She was often ill, but each time she went home and became well. How the lonely realization that she no longer had a home to go back to must have tormented her! That she didn't have many friends who could distract her from her loneliness was also part of her fate, even though it derived from her own personality. She committed everything to her love for me, and became remote from her college friends, one by one. She had only Satō Sumiko, of the

Agricultural Research Institute of Tachikawa, and a couple of others, as close friends. But even with them, she exchanged visits only once or twice a year.

During her college days she seems to have been quite healthy and engaged in sports, at times to an excessive degree. But after graduation she had constant problems with her pleurae and, within several years after marrying me, finally contracted a serious case of wet pleurisy and was hospitalized. Fortunately it was completely cured. But when she later took up horseback-riding at some exercise place, she developed, perhaps as a result of that, a retroverted uterus and had to be hospitalized again for surgery. She also suffered from appendicitis. She always had one ailment or another. The time she enjoyed good health the most was limited to a couple of years around the fourteenth year of Taishō. Even when she was sick, though, she was never depressing. She was always bright and calm. When sad, she shed tears and wept, but she recovered herself quickly.

It seems that she had her first mental disorders when I was traveling the Sanriku Region in the sixth year of Shōwa. I had never left her home alone as long as two weeks to travel; this time, however, I traveled on foot for nearly a month. From the stories of her niece who had come to stay with her and my mother who came to visit in my absence, Chieko appears to have felt the solitude acutely, and I'm told that once she said to my mother, "I'll die." She was then at the age to start menopause.

The following year, the seventh of Shōwa, was when the Olympic Games were held in Los Angeles. On the morning of the fifteenth of July that year, Chieko didn't wake from sleep. It appears that she had taken adaline after twelve o'clock the previous night; a bottle of 25 grams was empty. She was plump like an infant, with her eyes closed and mouth shut. I called to her and shook her as she lay in bed, but she remained asleep. She was breathing and her temperature was rather high. At once I had a doctor come and give her detoxification treatment; the doctor also reported the case to the police, and we put her in Kudanzaka Hospital. We found her will, but it had only words of love and gratitude for me and apologies to my father written in it. The sentences showed no trace of a malfunctioning brain.

After a month's treatment and nursing, she was cured and left the hospital. She spent the year or so that followed in relative health, but in time I began to notice various breakdowns of her brain. Deciding that travel might be good for her, I took her on a tour of the hot springs in the Tōhoku Region. But when we arrived back at Ueno Station her condition was worse than when we had left.

Her symptoms took one step forward, then one step backward. At first she often saw hallucinations, so sketched them one by one in her notebook as she lay in bed. She drew and showed them to me as they changed from moment to moment, writing down the time. She enthusiastically told me about the incomparable beauty of their shapes and colors. After a certain period of such behavior, she began to have periods of vague consciousness, and I began to help her eat and bathe just as I would an infant.

Both her doctor and I thought it was a temporary phenomenon during menopause. I moved her to a house on Kujūkuri Beach where my mother and sister lived, and had her take such things as Oba-Hormone. I went to visit her by train once a week.

In the ninth year of Shōwa, my father entered a university hospital with gastric ulcers and, after leaving the hospital, left this world on the tenth of October.

Chieko, at the seashore, became physically healthy and

got out of her state of vagueness, but her brain disorders worsened. She played with birds, she herself became a bird, she took to standing in a corner of a pine grove and calling out, consecutively for a solid hour, "Kōtarō Chieko Kōtarō Chieko."

About the time when the family matters following my father's death were largely taken care of, I brought Chieko back from the seashore to our atelier, but her illness then began to roar forward like a locomotive. I consulted Dr. Morooka Tamotsu as well. But she gradually began to behave violently, and, as she became too dangerous for home treatment, in February of the tenth year of Shōwa I put her in James-zaka Hospital in Minami Shinagawa, through our acquaintance's introduction, and left everything to the kindly and careful guidance of the director of the hospital, Dr. Saitō Tamao. Fortunately as well, Chieko had her niece—a gentle-hearted young woman by the name of Haruko who had earlier become a nurse first class—to look after her to the end.

My memory of Chieko's progress after the seventh year of Shōwa is still too painful for me to write down in detail. Still, during the latter half of her hospital life her condition maintained relative calm, and I would say that, while her mind remained split, her hands joyfully achieved with cut paper what they had once been unable to accomplish in oil paint. The paper cutouts she made, which can be counted in the hundreds, are truly her fertile poetry, her record of life, joyful plastic art, colorful chords, humor, and appeals of exquisite love. In these she truly lives in health. When she showed them to me during my visits with her, she looked more pleased than at any other time. While I looked at them, she smiled at me, bowed to me, looking very happy. On her last day she handed me a whole package of them that she had put in order herself and, while breathing heavily, gave me a faint smile. Hers was a face expressing utter relief. Washed in the fragrance of the lemon I had brought her, she left this world very quietly several hours after that. It was the night of the fifth of October in the thirteenth year of Shōwa.

THE NOBUCHIKA AND
THE NARUTAKI

I'd like to leave a word or two on a kind of beauty which will become extinct. It's the aesthetic sensibility of a *métier* permeating my body as inherited from my parent, to be sure, but it is already fated to become extinct, and it is proper that it is. Besides, from a grand viewpoint on art, its *merits* are almost negligible.

Quite understandably, the most important things for the artist are his tools. The brushes and ink of the painter and the chisels and knives of the sculptor are, for them, I would say, second only to their lives in importance. A brush used so long it has become a familiar part of the painter is, for him, a rare treasure without compare under heaven, and there are many stories about how a brush that looks dirty and pitiful turns out to be, for the painter, his life, his secret.

For me, the tools of sculpture are the most sacred things in the world and my most beloved companions. These things are reverently separated from everything else, and no matter what happens, I must protect them with my own body. When the situation was such that we had to expect bombings any moment, I put a hemp string around my late father's memento, his tool box (which was packed with knives), so that no drawers would slide out no matter how I held it. As for the minimum fifteen to sixteen chisels and knives that had become so handy I couldn't part with them, I wrapped them separately in a blanket, wrapped them again, along with the two whetstones my father had similarly bequeathed to me, in a large, thickly folded sheet, firmly tied it up with a tough Sanada string, and whenever the air-raid alarm sounded, I would sling this, which weighed about sixteen pounds, over my shoulder and jump out into the street, a canteen dangling from my hip and a fire-fighting bucket and hook in hand.

When my atelier in Komagome Hayashi-chō was finally burned down in the great bombings on the night of April 13 in the twentieth year of Shōwa, I took refuge in the air shelter we had dug in a vacant lot nearby, and the only things I took there, other than two large bundles of futon, were the tool box I mentioned and the knives and whetstones wrapped in a sheet that I hung from my shoulder. The atelier burned and collapsed right in front of my eyes, the fire quickly engulfing my books and the artworks inside, but somehow I didn't feel any regret for them; rather, I felt cleansed, my head strongly filled with the thought "I can make do as long as I have these tools." I even felt as if the tools were saying to me, "Burn them up, burn them up, all that old junk, all those old works!"

Later, the tools and the futon were temporarily carried to the home of Mr. Miyazaki Minoru, in Totte-machi, on the bank of the Tone River, then sent to the house of the late Miyazawa Kenji's parents, in Hanamaki-chō, Iwate Prefecture. After that house was burned in the war, they moved from place to place, finally settling down in this mountain hut in Yamaguchi, Ōta Village. Even now I keep the tools and whetstones in a state of readiness where I can take them out any time. This is because I'm afraid of the fires that occur frequently on the mountain.

The tools I always used and the tools my late father loved to use are, of course, mainly chisels and knives; other than that, there are a miscellany of tools for detailed work. One odd thing may be a pair of large magnifying spectacles of the sort Takizawa Bakin, of the past, might have used. They have a round cushion where the center of the eyebrow falls, and you put them on by affixing them to your ears by strings. These my father used for minutely detailed work, such as carving a Buddha's image on an *inrō*. It looks as if you could use these to carve things on a grain of rice.

The chisels and knives I have—both the ones my father loved to use and those I myself bought long ago—are all superior stuff of the kind you can probably no longer get these days. The sharpness of the chisels and knives that the smiths forged out of the best steel available, following the tradition that was alive until the period from the Sino-Japanese War and the Russo-Japanese War, can't readily be described in words. Among others, that of the type of knife called *kiridashi* (shaped like the one you use to shave dried bonito), which the smith by the name of Nobuchika hammered out, makes me want to say, "Fantastic!"

First of all, its shape is good. With a knife, by "front" *(omote)* we refer to its black backside. Both the black, viscous-looking surface of its base metal and the balance of the angles, the way both sides are shaved aslant, give the knife so palpably the dignity of a masterpiece. Usually, you make a knife or chisel by hammering an approximate shape out of base metal and then melding steel plates onto the "back" *(ura)* to make the blade, but the balance in thickness between base metal and steel, the balance in hardness between them, and other things greatly influence its sharpness. Because these things differ from smith to smith, each knife or chisel has its unique qualities.

The pieces made by Nobuchika have a relatively soft base metal, and the steel is made thin. If you sharpen one of these on a whetstone, the base metal "comes down" softly, producing black clouds in the water. With the impetus of the base metal coming down, you can sharpen the cutting edge of the steel just right. You take a look and see at the end of the base metal a thin straight line of steel blade shining white in supreme calmness. You turn up the knife to look at the blade from the bottom: all of it is of course steel, and it is flat and shines like a mirror. The shine is opaque. Somewhat white, it looks as if puffs of mist were hanging over it and doesn't glisten unnecessarily brightly. It has a faint suggestion, visible and invisible, of the "grain" made by the layers of steel when it was folded and refolded while being tempered.

I've been sharpening and using these Nobuchika knives for so long that some of them, originally five or six inches in length, have gradually become shorter and now have the name Nobuchika engraved on the back of the all-base-metal part emerging from the grip. These feel all the more precious for that. Other than the Nobuchika, there are the Maruyama and, near our age, the Muneshige. The Muneshige are much inferior.

The chisels and knives used for wood-sculpting are meant to work on wood, not to cut metals. For this reason they can be only several hundred times as hard as the wood and don't have to be unnecessarily hard like bits made of super-hard steel. If they're that hard, you can't sharpen them subtly, their sharpness becomes "heavy," and you can't use them. I've tested this myself.

No matter how good your knives and chisels may be, you can't get proper sharpness if your whetstones are poor. So the sculptor is selective about whetstones.

Even an ordinary person will understand the general importance of whetstones. It resembles the way the calligrapher prizes his inkstones, and anyone who has rubbed ink on the inkstone will remember the feeling. If you do the sharpening on a good whetstone, the blade "comes down" minutely and the cutting edge becomes extremely sharp, thereby improving the sharpness, naturally; you can also do the sharpening fast. Such a stone is closely textured but has sharp, minute points rising all over it. The sharpening can be done fast, but it doesn't produce a rough result. Such a stone is so soft as to suck the blade to it, yet makes the steel "come down" in quantities. The same is true of inkstones. With the ink made on a good inkstone, you can produce ineffable beauty in color and light when you "splatter ink."[1] Sharpened on a good whetstone, the blade comes alive, acquires the sort of dignity mentioned above, and begins to cut at will.

It has been said from ancient times that the *awasedo* produced in Narutaki, Kyoto, are the best; this assessment seems entirely right. An *awasedo* is a whetstone used to finish the sharpening; because it determines the degree of sharpness, it has been valued the most since the days of old. *Awasedo* are produced all over Japan, but none comes close to those from Narutaki. For this reason the Narutaki whetstones are called the *hon'yama* ("the quarry"). But the Narutaki quarry, already exhausted, no longer produces. Just like the Tuanchi inkstones, some still held by people merely change hands from time to time.

The two whetstones my father loved to use are both from Narutaki, one soft, the other slightly hard. Each has its own use. The four sides of each are painted in red lacquer, and each is encased in a paulownia box. One of them was a gift from Mr. Hirao Sanpei, of Rate Cosmetics, Inc., when my father made a wood sculpture of Mr. and Mrs. Hirao; the other he bought himself to celebrate the thirty-fifth anniversary of his service at the Tokyo School of Fine Arts. On the back of the stone is written "March 13, the 14th Year of Taishō." On September 10 of the same year my mother died. It is an unforgettable year for me.

At the moment I keep one of the whetstones in the gracious custody of Mr. Satō Takafusa, director of Hanamaki Hospital, in Hanamaki-chō; the other I keep right next to me in this mountain hut and use often. Whenever I touch this whetstone, heaven and earth become full and fertile, and this pitiful shack on a mountain suddenly begins to glitter as if with magic.

The wood sculptor by the name of Sekino Seiun, who was my father's disciple, had detailed knowledge about whetstones and had a number of good ones himself, but he died some years ago. I wonder what has happened to the superior stones he left.

Written this way, what I'm saying begins to resemble the stories about master artists, such as the one who made this *shamisen*, the one who made that violin. The chisels and whetstones, whatever they are like, don't affect what sculpture is all about. The Kuse Kannon [Avalokitesvara] in the Yume-dono was probably made without a whetstone from Narutaki. I haven't heard that Rodin had an outstanding burin. Brancusi probably works with files and paper.

In the end, the knives used so much that the engraved name of Nobuchika has come to be exposed are the symbols of things fated to become extinct. What is considered the primary beauty in wood-carving moves forward with the age. I've written this simply because I happen to know the beauty of some of the old tools. Such talk is a form of self-intoxication, and I don't regard it as unduly important. In sculpture, a far vaster untrodden world spreads before us, and has no end.

NOTES TO THE POEMS

Kitagawa Taichi gave much of the information in the following notes, directly through correspondence. Burton Watson translated the phrases and lines of poems originally in Chinese. Iriye Kyoko provided the literary sources cited. Unless otherwise noted, dates are of writing.

PART I: THE JOURNEY

The Country of Netsuke. December 16, 1910. In his 1929 version Takamura replaced Sangorō with Shūzan, a famous netsuke master of the Edo period, but in the later versions went back to the apparently fictitious Sangorō, presumably because it sounds better. "Monkey" and so on, in the last part, were all active swear words until as recently as the poet's boyhood.

Night in a Studio. January 12, 1911.

Desolation. March 13, 1911. Onogawa Kisaburō (1758–1806), the second grand champion of *sumō* wrestling, was often considered "tragic" for certain of the misfortunes he suffered. The "black star" in the fifth stanza refers to the black dot on the old lunar calendar marking the anniversary of the Buddha's death.

My Father's Face. July 12, 1911.

Italian Pilgrimage. Published July 1912. For "Tells Kapelle," see William Coxe, *Travels in Switzerland and in the Country of Grisons . . .* , 3 vols (London: T. Cadell & W. Davies, 1801). Mori Ōgai's translation (1892–1902) of Hans Christian Anderson's *The Improvisatore* (1835) was very popular; it is one of those pieces which Japanese like to think are better than the originals. For "honeyed words," etc., see Book 17, XVII, of the Confucian *Analects.*

Notes to the Poems

Complaint. Published August 1912.

Winter Has Come. December 5, 1913.

Clay. December 1913.

The Journey. February 9, 1914. As originally published, it consisted of 102 lines.

Autumn Prayer. October 8, 1914.

Clearing Sky. Published January 1917.

Cat. Published January 1917.

Melon. July 27, 1920. Leach is Bernard Leach (1887–1979), an English potter and Takamura's friend.

Cathedral in the Thrashing Rain. October 1921. As originally published, it had "Paris Fantasia 1" written at the end, but no 2 or 3 followed.

Wooden Clogs. Published April 1922.

From the Workshop: II. Published October 1924. Mrs. Yosano is Yosano Akiko (1878–1942), and Mr. Yosano, Yosano Hiroshi, her husband. Hiroshi was notorious for rewriting everything submitted to his magazine *Myōjō.* The persons named in the tanka are Ozaki Kihachi (born 1892), a poet; Yamawaki Kenjirō (dates unknown), a painter, no prince; Emile Verhaeren (1858–1916), a Belgian poet, many of whose poems Takamura translated. In the second and third tanka, *min-min* is an onomatopoeic name of a type of cicada.

Integrity. November 23, 1924. One of a series of poems on imaginary animals; the series wasn't completed. The original for "weasel" is *kamaitachi*, literally, sickle-weasel, which refers to "a cut in the skin from exposure to a vacuum formed by a cyclone" *(New Japanese-English Dictionary*, Tokyo: Kenkyusha, 1954), said to be common in certain northwestern districts of Japan. Apparently Takamura made more of weasel than sickle.

Polar Bears. January 19, 1925. When the poem was reprinted in *Record*, a book of his patriotic poems published in 1944, Takamura added the following introduction:

> Written January, 14th year of Taishō [1925]. In the 39th year of Meiji [1906], I was having a hard time studying in New York City, America. Since it was after the Russo-Japanese War, there was no more of the fierce air of the anti-Japanese movement several years before, but I constantly ran into people who made it clear that *they* had intervened to save our face. The Bronx Park in a New York suburb was my sole place of consolation. The animals never said, "Hello, Jap."

Head-hunting. February 2, 1925.

Onions. December 28, 1925.

Harsh Insight. February 28, 1926.

Comic Verse. March 1, 1926. Its first published title was "Comic Verse Given to a Certain Kind of European Poets Who Amuse Themselves with the Orient." The word "chic" is for *fūryū*, which, as used in the original, points to a somewhat dilettantish delight in polite arts, such as tea ceremony. The figures mentioned are Andō Hiroshige (1797–1858), a painter; Suzuki Harunobu (1725–1770), a painter; Matsuo Bashō (1644–1694), a poet; Yosa Buson (1716–1783), a painter and poet; Ike Taiga (1723–1776), a painter; and Sesshū (1420–1506), a painter. The phrase *hakushi no san*, rendered here as "praise on blank paper," is ambiguous. Through Mr. Kitagawa, Mr. Harada Minoru of the Tokyo National Museum has commented: "Toward the end of the Muromachi period there was a Kojima Ryōsen, whose *nom de plume* was Hakushi (white or blank paper), and he seems to have painted too. But unlike Sesshū and Taiga, he is not known to the general public. So I tend to think that in the poem perhaps it literally means 'a praise that is not written down,' and that Kōtarō meant it as sarcasm." The *Kojiki* (Record of ancient matters) is the earliest account of Japanese history, completed in 712. *"Japon"* happens to sound like an onomatopoeic Japanese word that means something like "splosh."

Gratitude. April 9, 1926.

Thunder Beast. June 12, 1926. Another imaginary animal poem.

Waiting for Autumn. September 27, 1926.

Big Sneeze. November 20, 1926.

Late Night. November 20, 1926. Toller probably is the German dramatist Ernst Toller (1893–1939), who had a book of poems, *Das Schwalbenbuch* ("written, 1923, in the fortress of Niedershonenfeld"), published in 1924. The Second Patriarch refers to Hui-k'o (487–593), who is said to have cut off his right arm to obtain permission to "enter Bodhidharma's room."

Mars Is Out. December 5, 1926.

Winter, My Friend. December 30, 1926.

What's Great. December 31, 1926.

Daybreak. March 12, 1927. The last line may allude to section 6 of Whitman's "Song of Myself."

Thinking of Mother. August 15, 1927. Throwing flint sparks over oneself was a traditional purification rite. Kōtarō's mother died in 1925 at the age of sixty-nine. The original version had an envoy consisting of two tanka.

Notes to the Poems

15 *Occasional Pieces.* October 10, 1927. As originally published, the seventh piece had "Chinese" instead of "great man."

Peaceful Time. November 20, 1927.

Tattered Ostrich. February 7, 1928.

The Natural Thing. April 9, 1928.

Alone Absorbing Oxygen. December 1, 1928.

"Falling Ill on a Journey." December 3, 1928. "Falling ill," etc., is the hokku Bashō composed just before dying.

Kitajima Setsuzan. April 20, 1929. Kitajima died in 1694.

Knife Whetter. June 5, 1930.

The Lanky Fellow Keeps Silent. August 13, 1930. The piece describes the celebration of Kōun's seventy-seventh birthday, which took place on April 16, 1928. What is said of Kōun in the introductory portion is fairly accurate. Takamura wanted the last line dropped; asked why, he said, "Because I couldn't do a thing, after all."

Portrait. February 6, 1931. The "catfish" is Baron Ōkura Kihachirō (1837–1928), who had a lot to do with the businesses of import, export, mining, construction, and public utilities in his time. The terracotta head that Takamura made out of the drawings is one of his few surviving sculptures. Despite the tone of the poem, Takamura didn't exactly dislike the man; at least, he was proud of what he made out of him.

Haunted House. September 24, 1935. The original for the phrase "boldly dropped everything, and let his spirit wander" is *hōge yūshin.* For the full four and a half years between "Portrait" and

Notes to the Poems

"Haunted House," Takamura wrote only sixteen poems—unusually few for a poet who averaged fourteen a year.

Making a Carp. June 2, 1936.

Shark. July 7, 1937.

Baboon. July 8, 1937. Kharakantha: "Kings of demons, kings of Asuras present when Buddha preached the Lotus Sūtra; described as rumbling like thunder, or stirring up the waves of the ocean" (W. E. Soothill and L. Hodous, A *Dictionary of Chinese Buddhist Terms*, London: Kegan Paul, Trench Trabner & Co., 1937).

Unprecedented Time. December 19, 1937. When this was included in *Record*, Takamura wrote the following introduction:

> Published January, 13th year of Shōwa [1938]. On July 7 in the 12th year of Shōwa [1937], the Marco Polo Bridge Incident finally occurred. The North China Incident was expanded to China Conflicts, and Japan had to fight disadvantageous battles while deferring to the nagging big powers called Britain and America, but at the same time won devastating victories in her attempt to break the dreams of anti-Japanese China. Even among a public yet to be used to battles, there were fierce patriotic sentiments, and the determination to win over hardship was being made.

The History of Making the Statue of Danjūrō. March 21, 1938. The ninth-generation Ichikawa Danjūrō (1838–1903) was a superlative Kabuki actor. Acala, Fudō in Japanese, is Tathagata's most important agent, who holds in his right hand a sword with which to subjugate demons. *Oden* is a kind of casserole with a variety of ingredients.

Sitting Alone. July 4, 1938.

Night in the Haunted House. September 14, 1939.

Carving a Cicada. February 11, 1940. Tempyō is a forty-year

Notes to the Poems

period in the mid-eighth century, a cultural high point in early
Japan.

Setting Sun. March 11, 1940.

Living and Cooking by Myself. April 13, 1942. When this was in-
cluded in *Record*, Takamura wrote the following introduction:

> Written April 13, 17th year of Shōwa [1942]. I don't feel sanguine
> about putting a poem talking about myself in a book of poems of this
> nature, but as a record of a poet's life at times like this I'd like to in-
> sert one. This is a poem I wrote when I was given the first Imperial
> Art Academy prize. My mother died in the 14th year of Taishō
> [1924], my father in the 9th year of Shōwa [1934], and my wife in the
> 13th year of same [1938]. Widower and alone. I sculpt during the day
> and write poems by lamplight. No disciple, maid, servant. One work-
> shop, three living rooms. I have a strong body.

The Pacific War had begun four months before the poem was writ-
ten, and the situation had become desperate when the introduction
was added in early 1944. Sen Rikyū (1520–1591) perfected "*wabi*
tea." Rinzai (Lin-chi: died 867) was a Zen master who founded the
Rinzai school. The "monk" referred to at the end is Ryōkan (1757–
1831). A calligrapher and tanka poet, Ryōkan also wrote many
poems in Chinese, one of which reads:

> In my sleeve the colored ball worth a thousand in gold;
> I dare say no one's as good at *temari* as me!
> And if you ask what it's all about—
> one - two - three - four - five - six - seven.

A *temari* is "a cloth ball wound with colored thread and used for
various children's games, among them counting games."

Beautiful Dead Leaf. September 18, 1944. Lines 14–15 allude to
the poem of Po Chü-i (772–846), "Seeing Wang Eighteen [Wang
Chin-fu] Off on His Return to the Mountains and Writing of the
Old Days at the Hsien-yu Temple," which has the lines: "Among
the trees we heated wine, burning red autumn leaves; / on the stone
we inscribed poems, brushing away the green moss."

249

Notes to the Poems

To General Kuribayashi. March 21, 1945. During the battle of Iwo Jima that began February 19 and ended in early April, 1945, about 7,000 Americans and all but 1,000 of the 23,000 Japanese on the island under Lieutenant General Kuribayashi Tadamichi's command were killed. Traditionally, Japanese military men wrote tanka before dying. To "be reborn seven times," etc., was a nationalist slogan, which comes from the last words of Kusunoki Masasue (?–1336); his brother, Masashige (1294–1336), was the greatest nationalist hero until the end of World War II.

The Snow Has Piled White. December 23, 1945. The original for "sea-fire" is *shiranui*, a mirage observed during the night on Yatsushirokai Bay, Kyushu.

Hunger for the Human Body. April 10, 1948. In Italy a certain form of cloud is called *contessa del vento*, hence the Countess in the 4th stanza. While in New York, Takamura translated portions of Benvenuto Cellini's *Autobiography.* The salamander episode occurs at the beginning of the book (p. 20 in George Bull's translation). Cf. Florence McCulloch, "Medieval Latin & French Bestiaries," *Studies in the Romantic Languages & Literatures* 33 (1962), pp. 161–162. The *Commandant* is General Douglas MacArthur, who was then the virtual head of Japan as Supreme Commander for the Allied Powers.

Hands Wet with Moon. October 10, 1949. Lines 3–4 allude to the poem of Tu Fu (712–770), "The Way Friends Treat You When You're Poor," which opens with the line: "A flip of the palm and clouds come out, another flip and it's rain." Line 9 alludes to "Lunar God," a poem of Miyazawa Kenji.

PART II: CHIEKO

To Someone. July 25, 1912. At that time Chieko had a marriage offer in her home town. The original for "Mother of God" is *Santa Maria.*

Notes to the Poems

Fear. August 1912.

To Someone in the Suburbs. November 25, 1912.

To Someone. February 18, 1913.

Late Night Snow. February 19, 1913.

Fountain of Mankind. March 15, 1913. Six months later Chieko and Kōtarō were engaged.

In Adoration of Love. February 12, 1914. Indra is the principal deity in Vedic mythology; the god of thunder and hail, later the god of warfare. In Buddhist tradition, stemming from the *Avatamsaka Sutra*, each jewel in Indra's net contains the reflection of every other jewel in the net and is likewise reflected in its entirety in each of them. Chieko and Kōtarō were married ten months after the poem was written.

Dinner. April 25, 1914.

Two Under the Tree. March 11, 1923. The tanka quoted at the outset is by Takamura.

Cattle on a Mad Run. June 17, 1925. What is described may have happened more than ten years previously.

Catfish. February 5, 1926.

Two at Night. March 11, 1926.

Child's Talk. May 11, 1928.

Life in Perspective. January 22, 1935.

Chieko Riding the Wind. April 24–25, 1935. From May till De-

Notes to the Poems

cember 1934 Chieko lived with her mother and sister on the Pacific coast in Chiba, and Kōtarō went to see her every week.

Chieko Playing with Plovers. July 11, 1937. See the preceding note.

Invaluable Chieko. July 12, 1937.

Two at the Foot of the Mountain. June 20, 1938. Hoping to improve Chieko's condition, Kōtarō took her to various hot springs in August 1933. Dr. Muramatsu Kōji says that "I'll go to pieces pretty soon" is a premonition common to schizophrenics ("Kōtarō Chieko no seishin byōri," in Yoshida Seiichi, ed., *Takamura Kōtarō no ningen to geijutsu,* Tokyo: Kyōiku Shuppan Center, 1972, p. 400).

Lemon Elegy. February 23, 1939. On October 5, 1938, Chieko died in the James-zaka Hospital. The original for "engine" is *kikan,* by which Takamura may have meant the "entire living structure."

To One Who Died. July 16, 1939.

Plum Wine. March 31, 1940.

Barren Homecoming. June 11, 1941.

Shōan Temple. October 5, 1945; revised July 1947. The "One Page on Salvation" *(ichimai kishōmon)* is a "one-page" commentary on the Jōdo sect by its founder, Hōnen (1133–1212).

Dream. September 21, 1948. The original title is *Fummu-teki na yume* (Spray-like Dream).

Metropolis. October 30, 1949.

Soliloquy on a Night of Blizzard. October 30, 1949. The original for "god's rhyme" is *shin'in,* excellence, superlative mind; I have chosen to render a set of apparent meanings of the two Chinese characters as they are. Takamura made final revisions on this,

"Metropolis," and four other poems on the date given and had them published in January 1950 under the heading "Chieko Poems: Afterward."

PART III: A BRIEF HISTORY OF IMBECILITY

The sequence was conceived in September 1946, revised for the last time on June 15, 1947, and published in the July 1947 issue of *Tenbō*. It consists of six parts and twenty poems: FAMILY, seven poems; MODULATION, two; REBELLION, two; HOLING UP, two; ANTINOMY, five; and BY THE HEARTH, two.

FAMILY. The original for the group title is *ie*, "house, home, household."

Kowtow. The word for the title is *dogeza*, "sitting right on the ground," a euphemism, considering that the person required to assume the posture had to prostrate himself with his forehead on the ground while the noble or nobles passed; it was a feudal practice which the Meiji regime (1868–1912) was supposed to have abolished. If Takamura's memory is correct, he was almost six years old then, for the so-called Meiji Constitution was promulgated and the emperor went to Ueno in February 1889; Takamura grew to be a tall, strongly-built man, but as a child he was feeble and unable to talk until three. At that time it was believed that if one looked directly at the emperor, a living god, one would go blind.

Topknot. Before the beginning of the Meiji period in 1868, the top-knot called *chommage*, like the pigtail which the Manchus forced on the Chinese during the Ch'ing dynasty, was the official hairdo. The crew cut *(zangiri)* then took over; a popular song at the time went, in part: *Zangiri atama o tataite mireba bummei kaika no oto ga suru* (Slap your zangiri head, and it plonks, "Civilization and Enlightenment!").

Lieutenant Gunji. Gunji Naritada (1860–1924), lieutenant of the Imperial Navy and explorer, organized the National Duty Society

Notes to the Poems

(Hōko Gikai) in 1893 and led a flotilla destined for the Kurile (Chishima) Islands. The shipwreck occurred on May 21 and was reported nationally as a tragic and therefore patriotic incident.

Sino-Japanese War. The war (July 1894–April 1895) was about a rebellion in Korea and ended in a series of Japanese victories. Harada Jūkichi was made a national hero for letting the Japanese troops through the Turtle Gate into the city of Pyongyang. (For an account of Harada, see Donald Keene's "The Sino-Japanese War of 1894–95 and Its Cultural Effects in Japan," in *Tradition and Modernization in Japanese Culture*, Princeton: Princeton University Press, 1971, pp. 151–153). "Mr. T.," *kore-sama* in the original (literally, "Mr. This"), refers to a supernatural being called *tengu*, direct naming of which was then considered blasphemous. It had a long nose and flew on wings. Kōtarō was called Mitsutarō in his boyhood, hence Mitsu for endearment. Kobugahara is a shrine nearby where the tengu was supposed to live.

Sculpting in the Imperial Presence. For having flints sparked, see note to "Thinking of Mother."

Funds for Building Warships. At that time, imperialism was rather blatant. Seeing Japan take the Liaotung Peninsula and other territories after defeating China in 1895, the "Westerners, far from condemning the Japanese for their aggressions, applauded them as being apt pupils. They also taught the Japanese how ruthless the game of imperialism could be and how unwilling Westerners were to accept other races as full equals. Russia, France, and Germany banded together to force Japan to return the Liaotung Peninsula to China, and then three years later these same powers cynically seized new slices of China, the Russians taking the Liaotung Peninsula for themselves" (Edwin O. Reischauer, *Japan: The Story of a Nation*, New York: Knopf, 1970, p. 147).

The Statue of Lord Kusunoki. For Kusunoki Masashige, see note to "To General Kuribayashi." The Double Bridge on Nijūbashi is the outermost limit of the Imperial Palace, where commoners are allowed.

Notes to the Poems

Sculpture Only. The Russo-Japanese War began in February 1904 and ended, with President Theodore Roosevelt's intervention, in September 1905. The "dire story of Port Arthur" most likely refers to the death of Commander Hirose Takeo (1868–1904), leader of a Port Arthur commando unit, who is said to have been hit directly by an artillery shell while searching for the last man on a sinking ship. In the "Japan Sea battle," which took place in May 1905, the Japanese fleet under the command of Admiral Tōgō Heihachirō (1847–1934) demolished Russia's Baltic Fleet. Japan had defeated a major Western power, and anything that showed Japanese equality or superiority to Westerners was capitalized on; one such example was apparently the "contrast" between Ambassador Komura Jutarō (1855–1911) and Sergei Yulievich Witte (1849–1915) at Portsmouth, New Hampshire, where the treaty was signed. In one photograph, Komura looks skinny, Witte portly. Ishikawa Takuboku (1886–1912) was a tanka poet. *Rojin* is Auguste Rodin; the mistransliteration is deliberate.

Cooperative Council. The man who urged him to join the Central Cooperative Council (Chūō Kyōryoku Kaigi) was Kishida Kunio (1890–1954), a playwright and stage director.

The Day of Pearl Harbor. Japan attacked Pearl Harbor on December 8 (Japan Time), 1941.

Romain Rolland. Takamura began translating Rolland (1866–1944) as early as 1911 and, with friends, set up the Association of Friends of Romain Rolland in 1926. Rolland had written an essay called "Above the Battle" *(Au-dessus de la mêlée)* in 1915. The "other color" of poems are those collected in *Ishikure no uta,* whose manuscript was destroyed during a bombing in 1945.

Imbecility. "They" apparently refers to the Special Secret Service Police, the Military Police, and other bodies that kept a close eye on the citizenry.

End of the War. Japan surrendered on August 15, 1945, and the emperor spoke to the people over the radio for the first time. Early in the following year, the emperor declared that he was not a living god. The Allied Powers revealed the atrocities the Japanese military had committed since the 1930s.

Report. The Allied Powers attempted to change every aspect of Japanese society.

Mountain woods. The original for "beating time on the ground" is *gekijō (chin-jang).* As cited in *Ti-wang shih-chi* (Chronicles of emperors and kings) by Huang-fu Mi (215–282), the song of *gekijō* goes:

At sunup to work,
sundown to rest,
drinking from a well I dug,
eating off the fields I plow—
the Emperor and his might—what are they to me?

NOTES TO THE PROSE

A Bundle of Letters Left Unmailed. Published in the July 1910 issue of *Subaru*. Takamura had returned from Europe a year earlier. Seven of the nine letters are translated here.

1. The 7-7-syllable words are apparently from a poem in the *Man'yōshū*, but I can't find the original poem. The phrase *shizuku shiratama* occurs in an anonymous poem (no. 2445), though Takamura has it *mizuku shiratama*.

2. Ironically (or otherwise), Takamura's upstairs neighbor at the time may well have been Rainer Maria Rilke, who was then working for Rodin as a secretary.

3. The reference is to Kuroda Seiki's painting that caused a great sensation in 1895 when it was unveiled at the fourth National Fair for Industrial Promotion. Entitled "Morning Makeup" and depicting a naked European woman facing a full-length mirror, it prompted the Metropolitan Police to send an officer to hide her genitals behind a piece of cloth.

Back from France. Published in the March 1910 issue of *Bunshō Sekai* as "Written as Spoken." One of the six sections and the first half of another are translated here.

A Last Glance at the Third Ministry of Education Art Exhibition. Published in the January 1910 issue of *Subaru*. The original article consists of eight sections.

Following the French example, the Japanese government started sponsoring an annual art exhibition in 1907 under the name of *Monbushō Bijutsu Tenrankai* (The Ministry of Education Art Exhibition), acronymously called Bunten. It changed its name a couple of times before 1946, when it acquired the name *Nihon Bijutsu Tenrankai* (Japan Art Exhibition), acronymously called Nitten. In 1958 government sponsorship was abandoned and the Nitten became an incorporated operation.

1. The 5-7-5-7-7-syllable tanka. On account of the total number of syllables used, the form is also called *misohito-moji*.
2. A sculptor (1884–1963) who studied with Kōtarō's father, Kōun. He won third prize in the first Bunten. Kōtarō's condemnation of Mōri, whom he must have known very well, is interesting because, in a sculpture show held less than a year before he left Japan to study overseas, Kōtarō himself had exhibited a piece entitled *Unfortunate Children* that had just the sort of theatrical storytelling element he frowns upon here.
3. A sculptor (1868–1927) who studied at the Berlin Academy from 1900 to 1902.

Ogiwara Morie, Who Died. Published in the July 1910 issue of *Hōsun*.

1. That is, "Michelangelo, Michelangelo."
2. The early, alternative reading of *Kō* of Kōtarō was *Mitsu*.
3. Jōruri chanting. The names that follow are those of the famous chanters of the time.

A Green Sun. Published in the April 1910 issue of *Subaru*. Written in a stiff, self-conscious style, with a sprinkling of English, French, and German words, this article was much talked about as Japan's first "Impressionist manifesto." However, as Takamura scholar Kitagawa Taichi says, it should be taken more as Takamura's attempt to clarify his own principles. The words in brackets are translations of the preceding words.

1. In Western art history, the term *local color* does not seem to include the meaning "regional color." The somewhat confusing arguments about the term on the part of the Impressionists and others may have led the Japanese artists to define it as Takamura discusses here.

Notes to the Prose

2. This may allude to Delacroix's observation, "Dans la nature tout est reflet" (In nature everything is reflected).

Thoughts. Printed in the catalogue for the second exhibition of the Fusain Society held in March 1913.

The Sculptor Mr. Gutzon Borglum. Published in the July 1917 issue of *Shinchō* as part of a series called "Impressions of an Overseas Artist with Whom I Associated Closely."

At the time Japan was having a windfall economic boom because of the First World War. A few months after writing this, Kōtarō, with his father's encouragement, announced a plan to sell his sculptures through subscriptions, with the idea of mounting a one-man show in New York when the war was over. Borglum was on the list of those who endorsed the plan, which came to nothing.

1. In a later account of his days with Borglum, "A *Help's* Life," published in the November 1929 issue of *Wakakusa*, Takamura wrote: "My work at the studio was from nine to about six o'clock. Every morning, as I arrived at the studio by subway, the first thing I did was to take out the thick, long hose placed at one side of the entrance and wash with water the pavement inside and the pavement outside, in front of the gate. You used no broom. Then I polished the door knobs and other brass pieces; oiled the floor of the studio; wiped things with a napkin; arranged the tools. At nine-thirty on the dot Mr. Borglum arrived from his apartment. Other than me, a secretary and an assistant worked for him. The secretary typed letters from morning to night."

2. In "A *Help's* Life," Takamura says he often quarreled with the woman workers of a hat-manufacturing plant nearby because they taunted him by calling him "Jap." "Once, because a gentleman hurled that word at me, I knocked his hat off his head with the water from my hose, and gave trouble to Mr. Borglum."

3. Borglum's "prize of the year," which Takamura received.

The World of the Tactile. Published in the December 1928 issue of *Jiji Shimpō*.

1. *Dairokukan,* the sixth sense, usually refers to the ability to

Notes to the Prose

grasp the truth of the matter without sufficient evidence or time to think.

Modern Japanese Sculpture. The last part of *Gendai no Chōkoku,* a lengthy, scholarly survey of the modern sculpture of the world, which was published in 1933 as an installment in Iwanami's "lecture series."

1. The Ministry of Engineering *(Kōbu-shō),* created in 1870, set up the department of engineering *(Kōbu-ryō)* in 1871, which became the University of Engineering *(Kōbu Daigakkō)* in 1877. The university was made part of the Imperial University of Tokyo in 1886.

Two Aspects of Realism. Published in the January 1937 issue of *Nanga Kanshō.* A transcript of a speech, the last paragraph is omitted in the translation. The original word for "realism" in the title is *shasei,* which is translated "sketch," "sketch from life," "copying of life," etc., in the text. The notion represented by the word is said to be traceable to the lessons of foreign artists invited to teach at the Technical Art School, most notably the Italian painter Antonio Fontanesi (1818–1882). It became important in literature as well, particularly in the tanka and haiku of the reformer Masaoka Shiki (1867–1902): hence, Takamura's reference to *shasei* in these poetic forms.

1. A Chinese painter during the period known as the Five Dynasties (907–960). Hsuhsi is usually known as the founder of a unique school of painting that emphasized *shai,* "the inner essence," over *shasei,* the faithful representation of the form.

2. A Chinese painter of the Southern Sung. Known for detailed depictions of landscapes and bold-stroke portraits.

3. *Takamura's original note:* G. H. Strats, *Die Darstellung des menschlichen Korpers in der Kunst* [The expressions of the human bodies in art] (Berlin: Julius Springer, 1914).

The Beauty and Plasticity of the Cicada. Published in the August 1940 issue of *Chisei.*

Because not many species of such insects as dragonflies and cicadas appear in ordinary guides to insects published in the United States, they are identified by their Japanese names in this translation.

The Latter Half of Chieko's Life. Written in September 1940 and published in the December 1940 issue of *Fujin Kōron,* it was made part of *Chieko Shō,* published the following year.

The Nobuchika and the Narutaki. Written on August 26, 1950.
  1. Or *hatsuboku.* A technique in ink drawing; with ample use of ink, it is used to draw shapeless things like clouds.

ABOUT THE TRANSLATOR

Hiroaki Sato has published a dozen books of Japanese poems in English translation. *From the Country of Eight Islands,* an anthology on which he collaborated with Burton Watson, won the PEN translation prize for 1982. Among his other books are *One Hundred Frogs,* a history of the poetic forms of renga and haiku, and *Nami Hitotsu,* a Japanese translation of John Ashbery's book of poems, *A Wave.*

Production Notes

Composition and paging were done on the
Quadex Composing System and typesetting
on the Compugraphic 8400 by the design
and production staff of University of
Hawaii Press.

The text and display typeface is
Compugraphic Caledonia.

Offset presswork and binding were done by
The Maple-Vail Book Manufacturing Group.
Text paper is Glatfelter Offset Vellum,
basis 50.